Peter Gill is a reporter with the ITV current affairs programme *TV Eye*. Among other African assignments, he has reported from Angola, Uganda and South Africa. Before becoming a television journalist, he was successively South Asia and Middle East correspondent of the *Daily Telegraph*. He covered the Bangladesh crisis, the fall of Saigon and the Lebanese civil war.

Peter Gill was one of the reporters who brought the Ethiopian famine to British television screens in October 1984. He subsequently returned to Africa on an equally important assignment – to examine the conduct of aid institutions whose task it was to prevent mass starvation. *A Year in the Death of Africa* is based on the documentation of these agencies and on extensive interviews with their key personnel.

PETER GILL

A Year in the Death of Africa

Politics, Bureaucracy and the Famine

PALADIN
GRAFTON BOOKS

LONDON GLASGOW
TORONTO SYDNEY AUCKLAND

Paladin
Grafton Books
A Division of the Collins Publishing Group
8 Grafton Street, London W1X 3LA

A Paladin Paperback Original 1986

ISBN 0-586-08537-8

Printed and bound in Great Britain by
Collins, Glasgow

Set in Times

Contents

Acknowledgements

I have been exceptionally fortunate in the people who have helped me in the preparation of this book. My principal debt is to two outstanding American colleagues who enabled me to piece together the United States response to the famine: Jack Shepherd, whose *Politics of Starvation* was the best account of the last terrible famine in Ethiopia, and Lorette Picciano-Hanson, who until recently was Africa Project Director for the campaigning agency 'Bread for the World'. In Britain, I am especially grateful to Oxfam and Save the Children Fund who agreed to open their files to me and then discuss all the matters raised with their customary candour. Although official aid institutions are notably less free with their files, I benefited from many frank conversations in London, Brussels, Rome, Addis Ababa and Khartoum. In particular, I would like to thank the information officers of the Overseas Development Administration and the United Nations in London, the European Commission in Brussels, the Food and Agricultural Organization of the UN in Rome, and the Relief and Rehabilitation Commission in Addis Ababa for their help in arranging appointments, answering queries and supplying me with valuable background material. Many people shared my feeling that this book had to be written. I would like to thank my agent John Lawton, of Curtis Brown, whose enthusiasm never flagged, and Peter Cutler, of the Food Emergency Research Unit, who brought his extensive knowledge to bear on the manuscript. All the judgements and any mistakes remain mine. Finally, it is very doubtful that my research would have gone so smoothly or my manuscript presented either intelligibly or on time without the interest and involvement throughout this project of Giovanna Forte at Thames Television. I am very grateful to her.

Glossary

I have tried to minimize the use of those confusing acronyms which litter the aid landscape, but these occur with some frequency:

AMC – Agricultural Marketing Corporation
CRDA – Christian Relief Development Association
CRS – Catholic Relief Services
EPLF – Eritrean People's Liberation Front
FAO – Food and Agricultural Organization (of the UN)
GAO – General Accounting Office (of the United States Government)
ICRC – International Committee of the Red Cross
IFAD – International Fund for Agricultural Development
ODA – Overseas Development Administration
OEOA – Office of Emergency Operations in Africa (of the UN)
REST – Relief Society of Tigre
RRC – Relief and Rehabilitation Commission
TPLF – Tigrean People's Liberation Front
UNDRO – Office of the United Nations Disaster Relief Co-ordinator
UNHCR – United Nations High Commissioner for Refugees
UNICEF – United Nations Children's Fund
USAID – United States Agency for International Development
WFP – World Food Programme

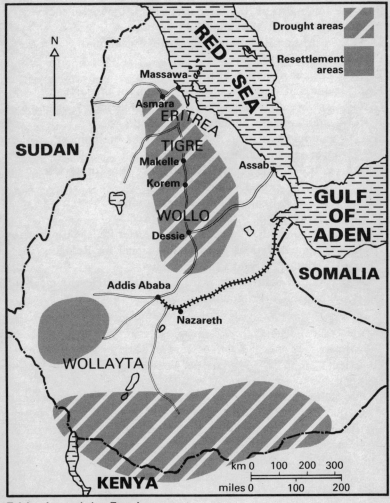

Ethiopia and the Famine

Prologue: Korem 1984

I visited Korem for the first time between 8 and 10 October 1984. No journalist had been there in several months. It was, looking back on it, a grim privilege to have been at the epicentre of a famine as deaths from starvation finally and grotesquely spiralled out of control.

A reporter should, or so I always thought, remain fairly detached from the events he describes. Emotion tends to cloud judgement. It is for readers and viewers to be troubled; it is for them to get angry and demand action. This precept I had more or less honoured in the past, and managed to hold on to during those two days in Korem. It is surprisingly easy to remain the dispassionate outsider when presented with barely recognizable distortions of the human condition – the scores of bodies laid out each morning for burial, the unnatural quiet of tin huts full of the dying, the misshapen form of the grossly malnourished. Even the numbers involved – tens of thousands in Korem – tended to numb the senses. I found that I could still just about cope with the dead and the dying. It was the despair of the living that finally put paid to my sense of detachment.

As I and my colleagues in the television crew drove away from Korem down the 2,000-foot escarpment to the plains, we stopped to film the hairpin bends beneath us. If relief was ever to reach Korem in sufficient quantity to feed all the people there, these would be the final obstacle.

Crouching in a shadeless ditch by the side of the road was a family. Like thousands of other families we had passed on the road in a slipstream of dust, they had finally, after years of drought, been driven by hunger from their land. Now they were struggling up the hill because they had heard there might be food in Korem.

The harsh grammar of television ruled them out as subjects for our film. They weren't quite starving enough, and there were only five of them. But there was a biblical beauty to that family that has remained

1

with me throughout my research for this book. The head of the family was a farmer whom months of hunger had robbed of sturdiness but whose dignity and resilience of character remained. His old mother was lame and could manage only to half-stand with one hand still on the ground for balance. They had been walking for two days and had the rest of that day to go. The farmer's young wife had a face that might have been framed by a halo. On her back she carried a male child who seemed the best fed of all. By their side was a little girl, dressed in rags and crying miserably to herself, perhaps out of hunger, perhaps out of fright at the business-like inquisition I was conducting with the help of a Save the Children Fund nutritionist and an Oxfam field officer.

I must have asked about the food that they as a family had had to eat. In response, the farmer lifted his daughter's ragged dress over her head. A pathetic, almost skeletal skinniness was revealed. The shock of her nakedness on the Korem road seemed to shame the little girl into stopping her tears. It shamed us into silence. There was little I could do for this family except give them a small sum of money to buy food if they could find any. Further questions were redundant.

Ten years before that experience on the road from Korem, almost to the week, I was witness to another famine. I remember taking the familiar taxi ride from the airport to the Intercontinental Hotel in Dhaka, Bangladesh, and seeing the body of a young man on the grass reservation between carriageways. The sight took my breath away, but I swallowed hard and directed the driver to continue to the hotel.

Bangladesh was part of my beat as South Asia correspondent of the *Daily Telegraph*. I was there first to write about the country's food problems triggered by floods in the North, and then to record the visit of Dr Henry Kissinger, United States Secretary of State, on his way to address the World Food Conference in Rome.

I have seen a British Government Minister heave an irritable sigh at the mention of Dr Kissinger's speech to the World Food Conference in 1974. In the weary, supposedly realistic 1980s, we should apparently treat the rhetoric of past politicians with reserve. But this is what the then Secretary of State actually said: 'The profound comment of our era is that for the first time we may have the technical capacity to free mankind from the scourge of hunger. Therefore today we must proclaim a bold objective: that within a decade, no child will go to bed hungry, that no family will fear for its next day's bread and that no human being's future and capacity will be stunted by malnutrition.'

In the autumn of 1984, as the extent of death by starvation in Ethiopia became apparent, Oxfam was running a particularly sharp publicity campaign based on Dr Kissinger's speech. It invited him, naturally, to eat his words. But the failure symbolized by the deaths and the desperation in Korem goes far beyond that of one man or even of one nation. It calls into question the credibility of a whole range of elective, nominated or self-appointed institutions whose fundamental task might have been to help prevent the extensive horror of the 1984–5 African famine. This book is primarily about those institutions.

Taking Ethiopia alone, no credible figures will ever be produced of the number of people who died of hunger in the 1984–5 famine. For their own reasons, the Ethiopian authorities are much less anxious to provide estimates of deaths than they were after the last big famine when the old régime was being called to account. It was then reckoned that 200,000 had died. This famine must have claimed at least twice that number, and experienced foreign relief officials in Addis Ababa say around a million may have died. I have no idea whether they included the family on the road to Korem, but I hope and believe that they were spared.

This study belongs to them. It also belongs to the thousands upon thousands of people in the West who were ashamed enough of starvation in their living-rooms to give with astonishing generosity to famine appeals. Only that response – not the television footage itself – shamed governments into making a respectable response of their own. And the more people gave, the more shamed governments became.

3

1

The Emperor's New Clothes

September in Ethiopia is the month of festival and celebration. It is New Year and springtime rolled into one. In the old days the climax came at the end of the month with the Feast of Maskal, the Feast of the Cross. Maskal celebrates the Finding of the True Cross by the Empress Helena, mother of the Roman Emperor Constantine, in the fourth century. It also confirms the great antiquity of the Church in Ethiopia, whose highland kingdom was converted to Christianity several hundred years before Saint Augustine arrived in England.

That was in the old days. Maskal is still celebrated, but today September has a different focus. Revolution Day is celebrated on 12 September, the day in 1974 when, after months of the 'creeping coup', a group of young army officers finally read the act of dethronement to the 82-year-old Emperor Haile Selassie, and the Ethiopian Empire ceased to exist.

The night before his deposition, Ethiopian television showed a film on famine in Ethiopia and the Emperor was under orders from his military tormentors to watch. It was called 'The Unknown Famine' and was reported by Jonathan Dimbleby. Made by Thames Television's *This Week* team, it had been shown in Britain the previous autumn where it had had something of the electric effect that BBC Television's news footage of another Ethiopian famine was to have a decade later. In Ethiopia the Dimbleby film is still credited with having toppled a dynasty that claimed descent from the union of King Solomon and the Queen of Sheba.

Before 'The Unknown Famine' was made, the imperial authorities had consistently denied reports of widespread starvation. They had closed down relief camps because they were attracting too much attention from the hungry populace. Even after the Government was forced to acknowledge the extent of the problem, it was dreadfully slow to respond. Not until the end of 1973 did appreciable quantities of relief grain get through to the worst famine areas, and one of the few gestures that the old Emperor made was to exempt the most hungry from paying taxes that year.

Dimbleby's report was a very powerful account of death and destitution in the north – almost too disturbing to watch today, even after the footage of the 1984–5 famine – but it was also remarkably free of any political message. It appealed at the end for assistance for Ethiopia and that was about it. No such restraint was shown when Ethiopian television finally showed his film. It was interrupted three times so that an announcer could tell viewers that the Emperor had refused to bring his personal fortune back to Ethiopia.

The famine had played a big part in the popular street agitation against the Imperial government. In the weeks before Haile Selassie's deposition, Addis Ababa had been covered in posters depicting on one side a weeping and emaciated child and on the other the Emperor throwing morsels of meat to his dogs. The famine had been a key factor in the destruction of the imperial régime, and ten tumultuous years on, Ethiopia's military rulers were preparing to celebrate their triumph in style.

The Masters of Ceremony for the revolution's tenth anniversary spectacle on 12 September 1984 were the North Koreans. Everyone who was there agreed that they did an excellent job. One senior Western diplomat neatly twisted the compliment. 'If the Ethiopians are looking for a 5th Brigade,' he said in a reference to the North Korean-trained 5th Brigade of the Zimbabwean army, accused of massacring the Government's opponents, 'then these boys will certainly do a good job in providing one.'

For weeks before the big day, North Koreans had been supervising the preparations. Huge triumphal arches were erected in the centre of town along the main routes that visitors would take. In Amharic and English they carried enlightening slogans like 'Long Live Proletarian Internationalism'. Hammers and sickles were everywhere in evidence, and over the central railway station hung the illuminated cut-out of a vast red flag. It says a good deal for North Korean workmanship that a year after the event these artefacts were still in place and looked set to remain as permanent reminders of the celebrations.

Artists of the social-realist school of Communist iconography were employed on big poster paintings for Revolution Square and other locations. Their main subject was Lt.-Col. Haile-Mariam

Mengistu, the country's leader who was depicted wearing a civilian suit and an uncustomarily jolly smile. Colonel Mengistu had his cheery gaze fixed on the middle distance, and behind him there were equally happy peasants and workers. The artists were left in no doubt as to whose achievements were to be honoured. Portraits of Mengistu dwarfted those of his supposed revolutionary antecedents – Lenin, Engels and Marx.

But the main task for the North Koreans was the parade itself and the drilling of 10,000 school children who were massed on one side of Revolution Square. In a meticulously timed display they held up coloured cards which spelt out revolutionary slogans in Amharic ('Down with Imperialism' and such like) and depicted the different insignia of military units as they passed the reviewing stand.

The parade was just under three miles long, and as such reckoned by those who record such things to have been the biggest ever. It outshone even the pomp of the fourth anniversary celebrations in 1978 when Ethiopia was marking its new-found military intimacy with the Soviet Union. Russian hardware had then flooded into the country to support the régime in its war against Somalia over the Ogaden, and within a month of those fourth anniversary celebrations the two countries had signed their Treaty of Friendship and Cooperation.

New uniforms were issued to the men who paraded in September 1984, and some of that Soviet military hardware was given a fresh coat of paint for the occasion. By 1984, Ethiopia had the largest and most sophisticated army in Black Africa and, given the number of internal insurrections and external threats, probably needed it. The leadership of one of those rebellions, the Tigrean People's Liberation Front, threatened to disrupt the tenth anniversary celebrations in Addis Ababa, and extraordinary security precautions were taken both inside and on the approaches to the city during September. Nothing happened, although it was reported later that in Asmara, capital of another insurrectionary region, there were bomb explosions during provincial celebrations and a number of casualties. In Addis Ababa, there was only one unexpected happening during the parade. As the military column trundled through Revolution Square, and at the point where some impressive rocket launchers were passing the review stand, the heavens opened and there was the most almighty downpour. For those relief workers and others whose job was to try and focus national and international attention on the dramatic build-up to famine in the countryside, it was grimly ironic that the parade should end in this fashion. Ten years before, an imperial régime had been toppled for its failure to cope with drought and attendant famine. As that event was commemorated in the middle of a far worse famine, the heavens had spoken.

Addis Ababa that day betrayed nothing of the tragedy that was building up in the countryside. Roads had been freshly asphalted. Every department of state, including the Government's own Relief and Rehabilitation Commission, had been instructed to devote part of its budget to sprucing up its office buildings. It was even said that beggars had been rounded up and carted out of town for the duration, so as not to offend the Revolution's visiting friends.

The roadblocks outside town served purposes other than keeping terrorists at bay. When desperate enough, Ethiopian peasant farmers and their families simply leave their homes and keep walking until they find food. It happened during the 1973–4 famine when the Imperial Government had been embarrassed by the arrival of people from the starving provinces of the North on the doorsteps of the capital. It happened again during September 1984. Refugees from hunger had marched for twenty days from Wollo and Tigre and were intercepted at roadblocks some seven or eight miles north of the capital. Continuing to Addis Ababa was out of the question, whatever the prospects of finding food there. So they were re-routed to a special transit camp, fed and then taken to areas in the south west for permanent resettlement – the beginnings of a process that was to stir immense international controversy in 1985.

If the starving from the north were discouraged from entering Addis Ababa, people in Addis were also discouraged from going to the north. Partly for security reasons and partly out of embarrassment at the prospect of two and two being put together to add up to Government neglect, foreigners were flatly forbidden to leave the capital. It was an order that applied equally to foreign relief workers and to journalists who wished to report on the famine. The senior Ethiopian official in charge of relief tried to assure me in an interview in 1985 that this ban had lasted only for a matter of three or four days during the celebrations themselves. That was not the case. It had applied for much of August and the whole of September. As far as the critical northern provinces were concerned, it had been in force since the beginning of August, if not before. Ethiopian relief officials,

7

diligent and effective though they may have been in many ways, did not control the issuing of travel permits to foreigners.

Mike Wooldridge, the BBC's correspondent in Nairobi, had been trying for months to reach the North. He had pressed for permission in June before leaving on a reporting assignment in the Gulf and home leave in Britain. At that time he attributed his failure less to official disinclination that he should see the famine than to his sharp reporting of a bomb explosion at the Libyan People's Bureau in Addis Ababa. Libya is a particularly close ally of Ethiopia, and it was entirely proper to wonder whom the Libyans might have been instructing in the mysteries of bomb manufacture.

Wooldridge was back in Addis Ababa for the celebrations, this time with a camera crew, and intent once again on getting to the famine. His technique, well tried by a generation of foreign correspondents, was to visit Government offices with upsetting regularity in the hope of getting a positive answer. If at first you don't succeed, wear them down. The answer remained an emphatic no. 'We've given you permission to cover the celebrations,' he was told at the Ministry of Information. 'You must do that. If you are interested in the famine, you must come back later, maybe in two weeks.'

He made the best of a bad job. There was some film to be shot of supplies being packed up for the North by Save the Children Fund and a strong interview with David Alexander, the SCF Field Director, who was similarly stuck in Addis Ababa. Then the press corps, more out of frustration than editorial enthusiasm, did the rounds of revolutionary press conferences. There were youth groups to interview, along with women's groups and trades unionists. They asked all of them about the famine, and from all of them they got the same sort of answer. 'The revolutionary women of Ethiopia are mobilized to come to the aid of their suffering compatriots.'

When questioned about their lack of attention to the famine during and before the celebrations, the Ethiopian Government can, like the foreign aid agencies, point to a certain number of things they *were* doing. The Relief and Rehabilitation Commission was established very soon after the revolution specifically to prevent a repeat of the ghastly famine of 1973–4. We shall be examining later relations between the RRC and the major foreign aid agencies, and charting the wholesale inadequacies of the international response. But what of the Ethiopian Government itself? How far was the Ethiopian leadership prepared to be influenced in its actions by the institution that it had itself created to prevent precisely what happened in 1984?

By March, it was apparent to Ethiopian relief officials that a major famine, with its accompanying death, distress and dislocation, could only be averted through massive Government and international intervention. Towards the end of the month, Colonel Mengistu left for Moscow. It is doubtful whether the prospect of famine was high on the agenda because the Russians were even keener than the Ethiopians to press forward with plans for the tenth anniversary celebrations. The anniversary was to coincide with the establishment of a new Communist party, the Workers' Party of Ethiopia, the first such institution in Africa. The Kremlin has always set great store by the Ethiopian revolution – Moscow's Cuba in Africa – and has at times shown itself notably more anxious than Mengistu himself to convert a military régime with revolutionary pretensions into a fully fledged Communist state. It is probable that progress in this area, not famine, was the subject-matter of the Colonel's discussions in Moscow.

Before his departure, there had been Government action on the growing emergency in the countryside. On 22 March a Ministerial committee was established which, according to an emphatic report in the Government-run *Ethiopian Herald*, would 'help provide immediate solutions to the drought problem now prevailing in the country'. Within its limitations, this committee of seven was responsible for a certain amount of activity. A sum of £5 million was authorized to purchase grain from Government stores to be applied to relief. Larger quantities of grain were directed to be sold in the province of Wollo, but this was of value only to those with the money to buy it. The committee naturally lent its weight to a major international appeal.

But as the weeks wore on, it became apparent that this committee did not hold the key to an appropriate Government response. For a start, Ministers in Communist administrations tend to be lowlier creatures than their counterparts in liberal democracies. Not one member of the ruling twelve-man Politburo was on the committee. Indeed, the committee's chairman, the Minister of the Interior, could not as a practising Christian bring himself even to join the ruling party, and despite his seniority was later in the year quietly posted to Sweden as Ethiopian Ambassador.

Major Dawit Wolde-Giorgis, head of Ethiopia's Relief and Rehabilitation Commission, assured me that the Government had

9

done all it possibly could to mobilize its own resources to fight the famine. Responsibility for the tragedy that struck with full force in the autumn lay with the international community, he argued. But I pursued with him the areas where I felt the Ethiopian Government was vulnerable, and his parting shot was this: 'I suppose you're just going to balance things up by blaming us.'

Ethiopia's Relief and Rehabilitation Commission has been described as a licensed beggar. It is encouraged by the régime to raise funds and food shipments from the international community. When an emergency strikes, its efforts to mobilize the Ethiopian administration itself are rather less welcome. I was informed that Commissioner Dawit did his very best to get the Politburo to respond appropriately to the emergency but that 'they just didn't want to know'. Commissioner Dawit was likened by one well-placed Ethiopian source to a leper, and as the tenth anniversary junketings approached, the RRC's isolation, by now both national and international, increased.

In the middle months of 1984, official attention was simply directed away from the likelihood of severe famine to the political priority in hand, the establishment of the new party and the anniversary celebrations. The last public references to the crisis, certainly the last utterances on the matter by Colonel Mengistu himself, were in June when the 10th Ministerial Session of the World Food Conference was held in Addis Ababa. Anniversaries fell like autumn leaves in 1984.

Mengistu opened the conference on 11 June. 'Ethiopia is currently suffering from the severe drought that has hit most African countries,' he told delegates in the body of his speech, 'and conditions are becoming worse even now.' It was a hopeful acknowledgement, but he then continued in rather less realistic terms: 'The revolutionary Government has taken immediate and concrete measures to rehabilitate thousands of people who had become victims of the drought which resulted from abnormal global climatic conditions.' There were no references to Government policy, no references to other environmental factors including population growth, no references to ruinous civil war in the worst-affected provinces. Climate was to blame. The Government was 'rehabilitating' thousands of people, which here meant shifting them out of the famine areas. Resettlement in less populous areas of the South West was one of the very few options open to the Government, but it was idle to suppose that it was in itself a solution.

10

The same month as the meeting of the World Food Conference, and well in time for the celebrations with all their important visitors, Ethiopian Airlines put the first of its new Boeing 767s into service. The airline was the first in Africa and only the sixth in the world to fly the 767. It commissioned two of them during 1984 at a cost of $60 million each. The arrival of the Boeing 767 enabled Ethiopian Airlines to extend its service to Moscow, and certainly made jetting from Europe to Addis Ababa much more agreeable for all the international aid officials and journalists who would eventually want to take a close look at the famine. Credit for the purchases was arranged through the United States Government-backed Export-Import Bank in Washington.

American business was not the only beneficiary of free spending in Ethiopia during 1984. A British company called Crow of Reading, which builds television systems, won a contract worth £3 million to improve television coverage in time for the celebrations. One result was that Ethiopians with television sets were able to watch the founding congress of the party and the military march-past in glorious colour rather than black and white. They saw nothing of the build-up to the famine.

In August a new television transmitter costing around £500,000 was opened in Makelle, the capital of Tigre, which along with Korem was to provide the most hideous of the starvation images on Western television in the autumn. This was described in the *Ethiopian Herald* as 'part of the revolutionary Government's ongoing media expansion', which in the words of the Minister of Information would enable 'the masses of Tigre region to follow the efforts being made for socialist construction in Ethiopia by watching television programmes on political, economic and social activities in other parts of the country'. Those activities did not include coverage of the famine.

Socialist construction was the order of the day as the tenth anniversary approached. Colonel Mengistu seemed to do little else during this period but unveil projects whose completion had been hurried forward for the anniversary. On 19 August, he opened a tractor-assembly and agricultural machine-tools factory. It had been partly financed by the Soviet Union, and the senior technicians who would run it had all been for training in Russia. Its direct relevance to the country's peasant farmers who remain responsible for the bulk of agricultural production was not immediately apparent. At full steam the factory would be turning out 1,000 tractors a month, but these

11

would all be going to the state farms which swallow up the lion's share of investment resources.

A few days later, Mengistu headed off to open a gigantic cement factory, this one partly financed by the East Germans. Three hundred Cubans had joined the Germans to build it. So thick and fast were these ceremonies now coming that Mengistu missed the next one, a textile factory in the heart of the famine zone, leaving it to one of his senior party men.

The Government received no financial help for the new Congress Hall where the founding meeting of the Workers' Party was to be held in September. That was a cash-on-the-nail deal with contractors from Finland. Colonel Mengistu had a particularly busy time of it that day. As well as opening what the *Ethiopian Herald* called the 'ultra-modern' Congress Hall with its 2,000-seat cafeteria, he also toured an exhibition devoted to ten years of revolutionary rule, and then opened the headquarters of the All Ethiopia Trades Unions and the new offices of the All Ethiopia Peasants' Associations.

United States officials who have never forgiven Ethiopia for turning its back on its imperial past have estimated the cost of the celebrations at $200 million. This is almost certainly an exaggeration. It also misses the point. The cost of the celebrations to the starving peasants of the North lay not so much in the money expended – the new Congress Hall is probably their only major directly attributable cost – but in the massive political distraction that they represented to the leadership.

Expatriate technicians working on projects unconnected with the celebrations describe them as having become an 'official obsession'. That obsession infected even the Relief and Rehabilitation Commission, which ought to have been able to continue devoting its time and resources to bringing assistance to the victims of drought and famine. Relief workers from foreign voluntary agencies in Addis Ababa say that on visits to the RRC at the time they would find office after office empty. Twenty-five members of a modest headquarters staff were required to attend the endless marching and banner-waving practice sessions that preceded the great day on 12 September. The same presumably happened in the regions.

Before Revolution Day, the Founding Congress was held in the Congress Hall. For Mengistu, it meant a new title to add to those of Commander-in-Chief of the Revolutionary Armed Forces and Chairman of the Provisional Military Administrative Council. He now became General Secretary of the Workers' Party of Ethiopia, and with the creation of the party Ethiopia became a Communist state. As the *Ethiopian Herald* put it, 'Let us be joyous.' The Revolution was passing to 'a higher phase of consolidation'.

The transformation was more apparent than real. The Provisional Military Administrative Council pointedly failed to dissolve itself despite the establishment of a parallel party structure. However enthusiastic Moscow may have been to see Communist power institutionalized in Ethiopia, it was as if Mengistu and his associates wanted it firmly understood that soldiers were still running the show.

The impression was confirmed at the party congress itself. Everyone entitled to a military uniform wore one for the occasion, and the new colour television cameras panned remorselessly up and down the ranks of braid and epaulettes. To cap it all the session was opened by troops in full ceremonial uniform goose-stepping down the main gangway. This was a military régime, the army remained in charge, and the people would do well to remember it.

Mengistu made two speeches at the Congress, one at the beginning and one at the end. In the longer of them, a five-hour affair in authentic revolutionary tradition, he made reference to the effects of drought, but they were not points that he emphasized. In my first reading of the speech I missed them altogether. He also pitched his observations at the level of pious exhortation rather than as urgent blueprints for survival. 'We must put an end to the problem that threatens the lives of millions of our people every time it fails to rain in parts of our country,' he said. 'From now on our slogan "We shall control the forces of nature" must be put into action. We must mobilize our collective efforts to free agriculture from the effects of natural disaster.' It seemed, once again, that only the climate was to blame.

Mengistu is not a popular figure in the West. Few revolutionary leaders in the Third World are. About the most complimentary epithet applied to him by the British press has been 'unappetizing' by the *Sunday Telegraph*. Certainly the right-wing member of the European Parliament who described him as a 'blood-covered buffoon with more than a million corpses to his credit' was overdoing things. Colonel Mengistu is no President Amin, no Emperor Bokassa. He is, however, a ruthless, dour and calculating operator, well described by one Western aid Minister as an 'intellectual thug'. Only a leader with those characteristics could possibly have kept Ethiopia together, kept a grasp on internal dissent, and kept himself at the top during the ten kaleidoscopic years of Ethiopia's revolution.

Mengistu has shown himself fully aware of the genesis of his power. He told a television interviewer from Canadian Broadcasting in February 1985 that the neglect of famine victims by the Imperial régime had been 'the cause of the Ethiopian revolution', and with some exaggeration added: 'It was this revolution which revealed to the world that hidden hunger in the North.'

At yet another opening ceremony on the day he became General Secretary of the party, Colonel Mengistu unveiled one of those imposing monuments to 'Our Struggle' which adorn Communist cities throughout the world. This one is in front of the main hospital in Addis Ababa and comes complete with an everlasting flame and a column with a red star on top. What is unusual about it are the massive bronze friezes depicting the origins of the revolution.

The villain of the piece is a feudal landlord on horseback, his appearance made the more sinister because his face is partly hidden by a bandit's kerchief. He is depicted rejecting the entreaties of his starving tenants. The portrayals of starvation are remarkably life-like and now familiar to every Western television viewer: a starving mother and her starving child; a starving father supporting a starving son too weak to stand. In the background bulldozers are at work removing the huts of the landlord's impoverished tenants. Tanks move along the skyline to complete a scene of oppression. How much better was the revolutionary response to famine?

It is not in hindsight alone that some parallels emerge between Haile Selassie's treatment of the 1973–4 famine and Mengistu's treatment of a later, more terrible one. Officials publicly reject such comparisons, of course. The revolutionary Government established the Relief and Rehabilitation Commission, so how could it possibly be accused of negligence? Relief Commissioner Dawit was emphatic on the point: 'In 1974 the death rate was the result of clear negligence and was the responsibility of the feudal régime and the aristocracy.'

Famine has been a regular visitor throughout the history of the highlands of Ethiopia. And Governments past and present must share much of the responsibility. The revolutionary Government of Colonel Mengistu has probably done more than any of its predecessors to bring assistance to the hungry, and its own Relief and Rehabilitation

Commission deserves to be excluded from the blame. But for the critical middle months of 1984, when much more could have been done, the régime decided to direct its energies and attention elsewhere. The observations of the Scottish explorer James Bruce resound over the gap of two centuries. 'The farmer in Abyssinia is always poor and miserable,' he wrote. 'To the problems of drought, floods and insects must be added the greatest plague of all – bad Government which speedily destroys all the advantages that the peasants reap from nature, climate and situation.'

2

On the Front Line

It is recorded that when Save the Children Fund first set foot in Ethiopia at the time of Mussolini's war in 1936, the locals could not for the life of them understand what all the fuss was about. The fund's initiative there had been entrusted to a formidable woman by the name of Mrs Lothian Small, who set about the establishment of what was described as a combined child welfare centre and emergency feeding canteen. The need was evidently great. Statistics were very inadequately prepared, she declared to the March 1936 issue of *The World's Children*, but she estimated that the infant mortality rate was as high as 600 per 1,000 – 'i.e. of every ten babies born, six never see their first birthday'.

On her return to England, Mrs Small told a meeting in Westminster about her experiences. The July issue of *The World's Children* carried this account. 'She found the people courteous and ready to co-operate. Nevertheless, they could not at first understand her mission, which was to help them set up some social welfare work on behalf of children ... They had heard of orphanages, but no one had thought of doing anything for the children in their own environment. Hence, it was difficult to explain that what she wanted to do was to improve the life of children in their own families. The Abyssinian mind, even the most enlightened, always came back to the idea of orphanages.'

From this discouraging start, Mrs Small's mission had turned into something of a success: '... it simply had not occurred to the Abyssinians that their children were underfed, and once they realized the fact, they were very ready to learn'. Speaking as one who had carried out a considerable amount of pioneer work, 'Mrs Small said she had never found any people more easy to work with.' The project had now been left in the charge of the Association of Ethiopian Women, thus adopting the familiar practice of 'starting an effort new to the country concerned, training local personnel, and then leaving

16

them to carry on'. Forty years later, the same practice was still being applied.

Out of Save the Children Fund's emergency work during the 1973–4 famine emerged an ambitious nutrition programme covering most of the northern region of Wollo, some 300 miles from Addis Ababa. Twenty-five Ethiopian nutrition workers funded by SCF worked through Farmers' Associations in the remotest corners of Wollo, their job to provide special care and monitoring for mothers and young children, often the most vulnerable members of the community.

During the few relatively good years between the aftermath of the 1973–4 famine and the onset of another, the system worked as was intended. Emergency help could on occasions be applied where it was most valuable, and the population sustained at home. But like the peasant communities themselves, Wollo is a region that lives at the best of times perilously close to disaster, and with the poor rains and the poor crops of the early 1980s a larger emergency was in prospect. People were once again on the move.

Korem is a nondescript town with a population of 7,000 on the main road that links Addis Ababa with Asmara, the country's second city. It has a small Orthodox church, a modest market, several extraordinarily scruffy hotels and an army barracks-cum-administrative headquarters. It had the distinction of being bombed by the Italian Air Force in the war that first brought Save the Children Fund to Ethiopia, but then the Italians bombed many nondescript civilian targets during that conflict. It is a modern war, between the central Government in Addis Ababa and the Tigrean People's Liberation Front fighting for regional autonomy, that marks the town out today. Korem is virtually the furthest north you can drive from Addis without risking capture by the guerrillas. Indeed it is quite possible that you will arrive in Korem only to find that the road behind you has been cut and that you cannot return. The countryside around the town belongs either to the guerrillas or no one, and that is why, as the last secure outpost on the road north, it is Korem that tends to attract a lot of hungry people when the food runs out.

Save the Children Fund can date the start of the great famine of 1984–5 to December 1982. It was then, in response to a growing number of destitute people arriving in Korem, that they opened their feeding centre for malnourished children. Between three and four

17

hundred children were cared for that month. By April 1985, the figure had risen to 35,500.

It is a wretched comment on our times that the selection of children for special feeding has become something of a science. 'Weight-for-height' is the basic rule of thumb for assessing how dangerously malnourished a child may be. But other techniques and measurements are being applied. In reports from elsewhere in Africa, there are references to 'MUAC' – standing for Mid-Upper Arm Circumference – a system which allows you to calculate how under-weight a child is without even having a pair of scales with you. Then there are formulae for converting 'MUAC' measurements to 'weight for height'.

Save the Children Fund in Korem adopted the tried and tested 'weight-for-height' method. First weigh your child; then measure its height; then calculate what percentage it is of its ideal weight. 'When it's below 80 per cent,' explains Tony Nash, a senior SCF nutritionist who worked in Korem, 'the risk of mortality rises quite quickly.' At the beginning in Korem, about a third of the children arriving in the town were below that critical 80 per cent level. As the months wore on, this figure was to rise to almost half. The severity of malnutrition was also to rise. Children were arriving as low as 70 per cent of their proper weight. 'Below 70 per cent you find they start dying like flies,' says Tony Nash in the deadpan tones of someone who has lived the experience. 'It doesn't actually get much worse than that. If they are much below 70 per cent you find that they die on their way in, even before they get to the camp.'

From the three to four hundred children being looked after in Korem over Christmas 1982, the figure showed a steady rise in the early months of 1983. By the spring, 1,000 or so children had been registered. It was then that Brian Barder, Britain's Ambassador in Ethiopia, decided that it was about time that this British project in the wilds of Wollo received a visit from Her Majesty's representative. By late 1984, Mr Barder was to find himself virtually a full-time relief official, but from early on in his tour he had taken a detailed interest in Ethiopia's relief problems and the contribution of British agencies in trying to tackle them.

Mr Barder was accompanied by his wife, another diplomat from the Embassy, and the Save the Children Fund field director in Ethiopia, Libby Grimshaw, when he set off for the North on 21 April 1983. After a six-hour road journey, the party arrived in Dessie, the administrative headquarters of Wollo and location of the gracious pre-revolution bungalow that acts as SCF's headquarters in the region. It was time for refreshment and a courtesy call on the Ethiopian regional administrator before pressing on to Korem.

The administrator would give no very clear reason for the decision, but the Ambassador was not to continue his journey. Was there a security problem, Mr Barder wanted to know? No, the administrator would not give the reason, but it was unfortunately impossible for the Ambassador to travel on to Korem. Mr Barder had arranged for all the travel permits for his party in Addis, and having driven for six hours it was a big disappointment not to be able to visit the British relief team in Korem. The administrator appreciated all this, and if she really insisted, Miss Grimshaw from Save the Children could continue her journey, but the Ambassador was to go no further than Dessie and that was that. It was as well, all things considered, that the administrator stuck to his guns.

At dawn the next morning the town of Korem was attacked by guerrillas of the Tigrean People's Liberation Front. It is probable that guerrilla commanders were working on very accurate intelligence when they ordered the assault that night. To pick up a Western ambassador in a one-horse town in the middle of nowhere would have been a tremendous coup. It is certainly true that the Government had intelligence that an attack was planned. Indeed, the administrator was subsequently taken to task for allowing even Libby Grimshaw to continue her journey from Dessie.

As it was, the TPLF managed quite a haul. In addition to the SCF field director, there were two expatriate doctors and a nutritionist from the fund, two workers from the Irish relief agency Concern, an American priest, and some Italian nuns. The fighting began at around 5 a.m. and lasted for about twelve hours. Shortly after it started, the SCF workers were taken from their hotel rooms in a compound across the road to the main Government compound, centre of Korem's defences. It was the worst place to have been that day.

The defenders could muster only 1,700 troops against an attacking force of 4,700. There was little doubt what the outcome would be. The Government had no real means of reinforcement or of counter-attack. The most they could do was to send in the air force, but by the time the MiGs arrived, the attackers were all inside the town and there was no way they could bomb and even be half certain of hitting the rebels.

19

The Save the Children Fund team spent most of the day flat on their faces listening to the fighting getting closer. Their nerves were not greatly eased by the regularity with which a Government soldier would pop his head round the door to tell them not to worry. At around 3.30 p.m., there was a series of massive explosions which they thought might be the last sounds they would hear. In fact the Government's ammunition dump next door had been hit and the rest of the defences now rapidly crumbled. Tigrean rebels rushed the compound and Dr Mahendra Sheth, the Indian member of the SCF team, courageously stood up to tell them in the fluent Amharic he had acquired as a child in Ethiopia that they were foreigners and not to shoot.

The suspicion that the guerillas were primarily interested in Korem's foreigners was strengthened by what happened next. Instead of hanging around for the eventual Government counter-attack, the TPLF 'liberated' what supplies they needed from Korem, including all the Save the Children Fund vehicles, and headed off with their expatriate captives in the early hours of the next morning. There were hair-raising aspects to this journey as well. First a careful watch had to be kept for marauding MiGs. And then the little convoy had to make sure it was following in the tyre-prints of the lead vehicle, because only that driver was certain where the guerrillas had laid the mines. The SCF team came through without too many fresh fights. Another group of captives was attacked by helicopter gunships.

Their ordeal lasted just over seven weeks. The first were spent travelling, much of it on foot with mules, their objective a forest clearing on the River Tekazze deep in guerilla-held Tigre, where the TPLF was holding its second Congress. It was here, too, that British television played a further part in the unfolding Ethiopian drama. A team from Independent Television News, led by reporter David Smith, had travelled from Sudan with the guerrillas to find the British captives. It may not have been Mr Stanley and Dr Livingstone, but it was a notable scoop, and Libby Grimshaw and the others were particularly grateful for the Scrabble set that Smith had brought. They were all released eventually at the Sudan border, with the TPLF banking on a certain amount of international credit for demonstrating that they could capture foreigners in the heart of Ethiopia and then set them free unharmed.

In Korem, the attack led to the abandonment of relief efforts. The children's feeding centre was closed down, and hungry families dispersed to fend for themselves. Save the Children lost everything they had in the town – important records and food supplies as well as their vehicles. The only tiny compensation was that among the food was a consignment of Bulgarian consommé for which nutritionists had been at their wit's end to find a use.

Even after the release of the foreign relief workers, it took time to re-establish the programme. Libby Grimshaw was by now in Britain trying to arrange a return to her post as field director in Addis Ababa. To achieve this it was necessary to acquire a fresh visa, and she had to pay many visits to disinterested officials at the Ethiopian Embassy in London. It was pointed out that her passport said that they had not left Ethiopia, so how could she possibly by applying to re-enter the country? When this sort of question had been answered, there were Ethiopian security officials in Addis Ababa who took an interest in her experiences behind the lines. It was not until September, five months after the TPLF took the town, that Save the Children was operational again in Korem. The passing of time had done nothing to diminish the crisis.

Within a few weeks of re-opening the feeding centre, the first 1,000 malnourished children had been registered for special care. By December 1983 there were 2,000 children registered; by early February 1984, 3,000. From then on the numbers began to spiral sickeningly out of control. Two thousand children were registered in the last three weeks of February, and no fewer than 6,000 children between 1 March and 23 March 1984.

The severity of the malnutrition cases was worsening too. According to SCF's records from the Korem camp, of the 6,000 children registered in the first three weeks of March, two-fifths were below the 80 per cent 'weight-for-height' measurement, and one-tenth below 70 per cent 'weight-for-height'. At that level the children were fortunate to have reached the camp alive at all.

During the months of heavy television coverage of the Ethiopian famine during late 1984 and 1985, the emphasis was on camps like Korem. This, after all, was where help was needed and had to be concentrated. But the camps themselves seemed somehow part of the scenery, part of the Ethiopian way of life – like the slums of Calcutta. This they most emphatically are not. Camp life is a final degradation, one small step short of death itself at the end of a terrible journey.

Hunger is endemic in the highlands of Ethiopia. Even in the best of years, peasant farmers and their families often do not have enough to eat. For three months and more before the main harvest in November and December, whole communities can go without food. This is the 'hungry season'. It is reckoned that only a fifth of farmers' activity is conducted in cash, and so they are astonishingly dependent on what they can grow. At harvest time their calorie intake is close to 100 per cent of recommended levels, their protein intakes well above. During the 'hungry season' calorie levels drop to 55 per cent, protein levels to 80 per cent. And this is during the good years.

The young and imperfect science of famine prediction should be set for something of a boom during the late 1980s. It would certainly be undesirable for a situation to continue in which major aid institutions respond only to public pressure in the West, in which the public in the West responds only to television pictures, and television producers respond only to the prospect of thousands of starving peasants dying in roadside camps. There must surely be a better method. In Britain, research conducted by the Food Emergencies Research Unit has pointed the way to an improved system.

During the build-up to the famine this Unit was conducting research in Ethiopia and publishing its conclusions in the journal of the International Disaster Institute, a body supported by the British Government. Like private relief workers in the field at that time, research workers were also frustrated by the lack of official response. Peter Cutler was one of them. 'I remember coming back in September 1984 and literally giving up,' he told me. 'We were just banging our heads against a brick wall. I'd tried all the donor agencies and the media. People were sick of my going on and on about it. Then along came BBC Television and everything changed overnight.'

What Cutler had been monitoring was what happened to families before they migrated to the camps, the intervening stages between the seasonal hunger to which they were inured and the despairing destitution that led them to throw themselves at the feet of strangers. A number of stages were tentatively identified. First, the menfolk leave their land to try and find work in areas that promise a crop surplus. Then the farmer will sell what assets the family may have for cash to buy food. Only when jewellery, farm implements and farm animals have been sold, invariably for pathetically low prices, will the family move as a whole in search of food. Perhaps the most pitiful sight on the roads of Wollo in the autumn of 1984 was that of men and women with big bundles of sticks on their backs to sell for charcoal or firewood. The sticks were the dismantled remains of their houses.

Difficulty in assessing the likely impact of successive crop failures on highland farmers led some knowledgeable people to predict catastrophe in 1983. They were out by a year. Put another way, the world had a full year's warning.

Dr John Seaman, chief medical officer for Save the Children Fund, who had earlier been closely involved in famine research work with the International Disaster Institute, reckoned in 1983 that crop failure had been so serious over the last two seasons that the next stage would be significant 'distress migration' across the international border into Sudan. In late 1984, it would be a facet of the tragedy for which the international community was unprepared. 'We got one thing wrong,' Dr Seaman told me. 'That was the level of capital reserves held by people in the highlands. We underestimated their cattle reserves, and the result was that people held out rather longer than expected. We expected distress migrations from November–December 1983 to February–March 1984 at around 150,000. In fact the figure was around 50,000. Nevertheless, by December 1983, it was no longer an "if"; it was simply a "when".'

Predictions from the relief agencies and the efforts of researchers to understand the workings of the complex phenomenon of famine were not just straws in the wind during 1983 and early 1984. There was significant death from starvation as well, though apparently not enough of it nor forcefully enough reported to stir the major donors into decisive action.

Perhaps the problem is one of language. Left to itself, officialdom the world over has a matchless way with words. 'If you can't quite remember what "starvation" is – bring in an international expert and he will tell you,' G. N. Vogel, former executive director of the UN's World Food Programme once observed. 'It's to do with "groups of the population which, because of insufficient income or for other reasons, were previously prevented from translating an inherent need for food into actual consumption".'

The approach of the journalist who tries to dream up fresh ways of presenting perennial problems is surely preferable. When the full horror of suffering in Kampuchea was revealed after the intervention of Vietnamese forces in 1979, *Time* magazine reported: 'There is nothing ennobling about death by starvation ... Soon after food is cut off, the body switches to burning fuel reserves in the liver and fatty tissues. After fat is exhausted, the body accelerates the breakdown of protein in the muscles, including the heart, which saps strength. At the same time the body attempts to husband its resources by cutting energy requirements to the minimum. Pulse rate and blood pressure fall and body temperature drops. Men become impotent; women stop menstruating and nursing mothers fail to produce milk; children stop growing ... Death comes in many ways. The intestinal walls become damaged, severe and constant diarrhoea may develop ...'* It is a text that could usefully have been framed and hung on walls in Addis Ababa and around the world as news arrived of starvation not just in Korem, but in Gondar, in Makelle, and finally in early 1984 in the deceptively verdant area of Wollayta, south of the capital.

I have heard it argued in Addis and elsewhere that the relief agencies did not do enough in the build-up to famine to bring their experiences in the field to the attention of Governments and international bodies. This is a pretty feeble excuse. From March 1983, for instance, Oxfam was producing regular monthly bulletins on the situation. Michael Miller, a former Oxfam field director in Addis Ababa, reported on a trip to Gondar in September 1983: 'It was a bad surprise, on arrival on the outskirts of the town, to see large numbers of people, sitting or standing in groups, waiting for grain distribution.'

Gondar had been giving concern for months. During the summer the *Washington Post* had carried a series of articles by their correspondent Jay Ross that began by quoting Trevor Page, senior emergencies officer for the World Food Programme, as saying that between 50 and 100 children were dying daily in northern Ethiopia. Ross travelled to a place called Zwi Hamusit, 52 miles from Gondar, where he reported that 150 children had been buried in the course of April and May. And here he quoted Major Dawit of the Relief and Rehabilitation Commission as saying that unless there was enough international assistance, thousands of people would soon stream out of the mountains seeking food. 'It will take years to rehabilitate them,' said Dawit. It was a central point – the need to keep people on the land – and the world ignored it.

In Addis Ababa, since the time of the famine in the early 1970s,

*Quoted in William Shawcross, *The Quality of Mercy*, André Deutsch, London, 1984.

there has been an agency co-ordinating the work of the voluntary agencies in Ethiopia. Called the Christian Relief and Development Association, it is run by Brother Augustine 'Gus' O'Keeffe, an engaging Irishman who has now developed a compendious knowledge of the country's transport problems and practices. Again, I have been told that the CRDA did not do enough to bring the full enormity of what was under way in the countryside to international attention.

The CRDA holds regular monthly meetings which receive, among other things, detailed accounts of agency work and experience in the field. These meetings were attended as often as not during this period by diplomats from the United States and British Embassies, as well as by representatives of the major United Nations agencies.

At the CRDA meeting on 7 November 1983, representatives from the American private agency Catholic Relief Services reported on a visit to Makelle, in Tigre: 'The rains had already stopped and it was widely felt that if the area did not have another two to three days of rain, the crops would fail. More recent reports are now predicting a 90 per cent crop failure this harvest season.' At the following month's meeting the experienced Brother O'Keeffe reported on his own visit to Makelle. According to the businesslike minutes of the meeting, his observations were to the point: 'As there had been very little rain in the area it is anticipated that the food situation will deteriorate during the coming year.'

The further development that should have raised alarm was starvation in Wollayta, in the more fertile south of the country. Here the Ethiopian Government had played a notably unhelpful part by levying heavy taxes after the 1983 harvest. It is said that they needed the money in good time for the tenth anniversary junketings. 'In many cases people had to sell grain, household goods, tools and animals to pay these taxes,' reported Hugh Goyder, Oxfam's field director who was skilfully to steer the agency through its response to the 1984–5 famine. After the taxes, fresh disasters struck. The short winter rains, which would normally be relied upon to provide a 'bridging' crop in the long wait for the main harvest due later in 1984, failed, and the root crop 'enset' known as 'false banana' was then attacked by disease. Oxfam had some important development projects in Wollayta, and were able to bring emergency relief to bear during 1984. But in that spirit of critical self-examination which is virtually absent in the official relief agencies (self-justification should on no account be

25

confused with self-criticism), Oxfam felt that it could have done better. 'In retrospect, Oxfam should have moved in much earlier,' wrote Hugh Goyder, 'and placed less reliance on the judgements of our long-established projects in areas which, it transpired, knew too little about the growing hunger on their own doorsteps until it was too late.'

Oxfam sent nurses and nutritionists to Wollayta. For them the failure to move more quickly took on a human face. One volunteer summed things up in a letter back to Britain: 'A sense of despair appears to have struck the people while we ourselves often become very depressed when daily witnessing the continual ritual of funerals in every village, the sheer misery of the aged, the cry for help from the young.' What was happening in Wollayta was by now part of a much larger mosaic of misery in Ethiopia.

It may be pointless to debate exactly when widespread death from starvation in Ethiopia became inevitable. What is certainly true is that the Western world – Governments, media, international aid organizations, and many private relief agencies – responded only when people were dying, not to the warning signals and not to the challenge of trying to avert famine. As Berhane Gizaw, head of early warning for the Ethiopian Relief and Rehabilitation Commission, put it to me: 'We allowed them to exhaust all their resources during the bad years of 1982 and 1983, and then left them to face the crisis of 1984 in that state.'

When I visited the relief camp at Korem in October 1984, the Ethiopian official in charge gave me two scrappy pieces of paper. One was an appeal for help and a list of the materials, primarily food grain, that he needed to keep people alive. The other, copied from the notebook that he kept constantly under his arm, was a list of the numbers dying in the camp month by month and day by day from July 1983. Up to March 1984, the monthly death toll kept to under 100; then it shot up. In April the camp recorded 854 deaths, and by October I returned to Addis with figures which were news both to Ethiopian relief officials and to the United Nations – that deaths from starvation in Korem had just topped 100 a day for the first time.

More assistance at any time before the TV cameras brought the camp at Korem into the front room would have saved lives. And if the private relief agencies that are now so cordially fêted by their big brothers had been taken a little more at their word at the time, catastrophe could have been averted. At the end of a year that had seen her captured by rebels, released and returned to her post as Save the Children Fund's field director in Addis, Libby Grimshaw wrote to her head office in London: 'We are going to have trouble here in Ethiopia in the coming year because of crop failure, food shortage, movement of people and all the usual elements that are part of life in Ethiopia.' She was particularly anxious about areas caught up in Ethiopia's civil wars: 'Our problem is to prepare ourselves for a disaster which we may not be able to do anything about.'

But the obstacles in the way of effective relief were not going to stop Save the Children in Ethiopia doing its best. 'I should also like to ask you or anyone else in an influential position,' Libby continued, 'to encourage donors – especially Governments – to supply ICSM [Instant Corn Soya Mix] and high-protein biscuits and oil, all of which are extremely useful and can be stock-piled.' At the end of this prophetic letter, she checked herself for an instant. 'Perhaps I am being over-pessimistic about the coming year …' she said. On the contrary, she had seen the future with troubling clarity.

3

Crying Wolf?

On office calendars in the Addis Ababa headquarters of the Relief and Rehabilitation Commission, 30 March 1984 was marked as a red-letter day. This was the date on which the RRC issued its request for emergency food aid to cover the rest of the year. In Ethiopia's crop cycle much is already clear by the end of March. A full assessment of the previous year's main crop is possible, there are firm indications as to whether the 'small' rains due to start around February will provide any sort of 'bridging' crop, and fairly realistic calculations can thus be made about how much food assistance will be required from abroad to keep the population fed until the next main crop in December. That, at least, is the theory.

The 30 March meeting was held in a conference room at the Ghion Hotel, just off Revolution Square. Like almost everything else in Addis Ababa, the Ghion is Government-owned and it was the regular choice for such meetings. It lacks the showy ostentation – and the expense – of the Hilton, which is also Government-owned, but enjoys all the services of a major hotel.

Anyone who was anyone in the Ethiopian aid business was at the Ghion that day. Representatives of the major United Nations agencies drove the half-mile from their tower-block offices, the tallest in the city. As the headquarters of the United Nations Economic Commission for Africa, Addis is probably the most important United Nations centre on the continent. The key Western nations were also represented at the meeting. Addis is the headquarters of the Organization of African Unity, and thus an important diplomatic crossroads. Of the rich Western nations, only Denmark and Norway do not have embassies among the eucalyptus woods in the hills above Addis.

The RRC holds regular 'donor' meetings, several a year in the recent past, and some donor representatives have tried to persuade me that

28

there was nothing out of the ordinary about the 30 March meeting. There were in fact several unusual aspects to the presentation that day as the RRC struggled to bring international attention to bear on the developing tragedy. First they showed the donors a film, a video compilation stitched together in part from Western television coverage of famine conditions, with an RRC commentary stuck on top. The question-and-answer session after the main presentation was particularly lengthy as donors queried the level of Government food stocks in the country and the capacity of the ports to handle large quantities of aid. Whether out of deference to the donors or to the recipients of aid, the press was excluded from this part of the proceedings.

Some observers also noted a change of tone over previous meetings. 'This was not just a ritual call for more assistance,' said Peter Cutler, of the Food Emergencies Research Unit. 'There had been a big change. This time they were really desperate.'

The document presented to donors at the Ghion Hotel was called simply 'Assistance Requirements 1984'. With what I consider to be admirable clarity, it spelt out the situation that Ethiopia faced, and then made a measured and coherent appeal for help. Had it been taken seriously, many lives would have been saved.

The RRC's alarm at the deterioration of the food supply position in the countryside was registered early on in the report. 'At the moment, only three months after their harvest in some cases, people have become forced to depend on outside sources of grain assistance.' Several regions of the country had not had rain for three consecutive crop seasons and this had led 'to large-scale suffering because drought always affects the section of the population least prepared to face it, i.e. the marginal and subsistence farmers'.

The report should have left the donors in no doubt that Ethiopia was now throwing itself fully upon international charity. 'The only alternative left to the country is to appeal for international assistance to bring relief to the population until such time as weather conditions improve and full agricultural production commences once again.'

After producing its estimates of the number of people affected in different regions (1,790,000 out of 2,500,000 in Wollo; 1,300,000 out of 2,400,000 in Tigre), the report began to spell out what would happen without major international assistance. 'Ethiopia is facing a potential disaster of considerable magnitude in which, this year, around one-fifth of the country's population will need assistance in some form or another. If those affected do not receive relief assistance, the consequences will be frightening.'

'Assistance Requirements 1984' ended with these dignified and eloquent observations, written, of course, in English, a language whose force can more readily be understood by the donors than by the recipients in Ethiopia. 'What the data cannot show and what must be very clearly understood,' said the report, 'is the amount and extent of individual suffering of families and their children and sometimes of whole communities. The marginal existence of many of these families even in good years and their helplessness in the face of harsh climatic and natural conditions is hard to imagine ... the magnitude of the problem this year demonstrates that Ethiopia must once again appeal with all seriousness to its donors for assistance in the prevention of a major tragedy.'

For an honest appraisal of why this report yielded such pitiful results, there was little point in my turning to the major aid bureaucracies. Their first response was to provide lists of what they had been doing beforehand, and then elaborate upon those with dark murmurings about Ethiopian unreliability. One of the few studies that really tried to examine what had gone wrong was a confidential report on the early stages of the famine prepared by Tony Vaux, an Oxfam disasters officer. Vaux is blunt. 'Virtually no one, including Oxfam, took the request very seriously,' he concluded.

He identified part of the problem as statistical. It was true that there were certain inconsistencies in the figures, and calculations based on the northern provinces of Eritrea and Tigre were unreliable since the Government controlled only the major towns – not even all of them – and only a fraction of the countryside. My reading of RRC documentation, however, is rather more charitable than Tony Vaux's. The compilers produced overall figures for Eritrea and Tigre, but were honest enough in all their supporting documents (also available to donors) to say that they had received no formal reports from either region. Later in the year the RRC made no bones about the peculiarity of the problems it faced in Tigre. 'Unless immediate action is taken, the crops failure coupled with the security problem in the region could make the whole situation disastrous.'

Any gaps in the Commission's accounting were, moreover, compensated for within the appeal itself. The RRC calculated that the country needed 900,000 tonnes of grain for the rest of 1984. Subsequent assessments by the United Nations were to confirm that this figure was spot-on, indeed rather below what the international community was eventually to commit to Ethiopia after media attention had prodded the big donors into belated action later in the year. But in March the RRC acknowledged that it would not be able to distribute 900,000 tonnes even if it were all delivered. It had to be admitted, the report said, 'that it would be highly improbable that the Commission would be able to distribute this amount of grain with its present limited resources'. It would also be very difficult for people living in remote areas with pack animals weakened by drought to reach Government centres for their relief supplies – perhaps a diplomatic way of acknowledging that the Government's writ did not run very far in Eritrea and Tigre. In any event, the Relief and Rehabilitation Commission appealed not for the 900,000 tonnes that it believed the country needed, but for half that figure, 450,000 tonnes, which it believed it could distribute. It was, according to some, a fateful error, and started that process by which the big donors could wriggle from whatever sense of obligation they may have felt.

Oxfam's evaluation report dealt first with its own response. After the donors' meeting, Hugh Goyder, the agency's field director, wrote to headquarters: 'There does not seem much Oxfam can do about the huge requirements for relief claimed in this report.' Goyder's comments were passed to Oxfam's Disasters Office and to the press office with a note saying that the Relief and Rehabilitation Commission report was available if needed. 'In retrospect, and bearing in mind that 1983 had been a famine year,' wrote Tony Vaux in the Oxfam assessment, 'this was a very low-key response, although it must be remembered that at the time Oxfam had no special funds for large-scale grain purchases.'

So what of those who did have the funds – and the grain – to assist Ethiopia? It was here that I heard from all sides that the Ethiopians had cried wolf before. Tony Vaux described the process: 'It appears that the constant repetition of appeals had produced a sense of scepticism which was not based on any past failure of the RRC's predictions but more a feeling that they were constantly asking for more. Agencies were tired of helping a Government that seemed to do so little to help itself ... With hindsight, one can say that the donors should have forgotten their frustrations and thought of the suffering

31

people of Ethiopia, not its Government, but one can understand to some extent the climate of inertia that gripped Addis in the coming months, especially as the Government switched its resources into the massive celebrations for the 10th Anniversary of the Revolution which took place in September.'

The notion that Ethiopia had cried wolf before was a poor substitute for argument. At its most cynical, it allowed donors to justify inaction in 1984 because not quite enough people had died of starvation in 1983. Worse, I have heard the same argument applied to the number of deaths in 1984. A senior official from the United Nations World Food Programme began by acknowledging that the aid community had underestimated the cumulative effect of drought and the extent to which people had disposed of their assets to buy food. He went on to state that Ethiopia started every crop year with some two and a half million paupers, as if that somehow absolved the world from efforts to assist them. 'How many do you think died in 1984?' he asked me. 'I would fervently hope that it was less than one million. But, frankly, to have believed those March figures from the RRC, there should have been three million dead.'

At no stage in the 30 March presentation did the Commission commit itself to a figure of how many would die. Indeed, at one point the report held out the dim prospect of an improvement in time at least to guarantee a respectable harvest later in the year. 'Should weather conditions change and result in an improvement in rainfall, it is hoped many of those now affected will be able to support themselves later in the year.' It continued in this sober fashion: 'This of course cannot be predicted and therefore contingency plans have to be made in the event that the drought continues.'

The appeal for assistance contained in the Commission's report was reinforced in a speech by the Commissioner, Major Dawit Wolde-Giorgis. Five million people were expected to face food shortages in thirteen of the country's regions, he said. Oxen would certainly die in the continuing drought, and that would mean that there would be no ploughing. 'A potentially disastrous situation, which demands urgent action, is developing,' he said. He underlined the appeal for food assistance and commended the RRC's own conclusion that $50 million was required for help with transport so that the 450,000 tonnes could be effectively distributed. It was a request worth recalling in 1985 as aid workers beat their breasts over the inadequacies of the

32

Government's transport efforts. At the very end of his speech, Commissioner Dawit did issue a specific warning about deaths. 'I would like to emphasize the gravity of the present drought situation,' he declared. 'Unless we are able to provide the assistance required immediately the number of affected people we have today could easily become a statistic of mortality tomorrow.'

Dawit is a pugnacious, barrel-chested individual who upset many donors with a directness of manner that bordered on rudeness. Ministers and officials in the West were the more put out since they were under the impression that he had come to ask for their help. He defied categorization as either of those two better-known Third World suppliants – the man with the begging-bowl and a bit of gratitude, or the man with the Ph.D who thinks it is all the fault of colonialism anyway. Commissioner Dawit put blunt and unapologetic emphasis on his country's requirements, and then produced an unnerving moral equation between rich Governments in the West and the miserable poor in his own country. It was a formula that seemed at times to exclude his own government from further obligation.

His approach did little to endear him to his natural allies among the voluntary agencies. On his first visit to Britain as Commissioner in 1983, he was accompanied on his appointments by his brother, who was then Ethiopian Ambassador in London. One senior charity official wrote at the time: 'Dawit was aggressively arrogant and lacked the charm of his brother, which lost him a good deal of sympathy with both the Government and non-Government groups here in London.' Dawit's refusal to flatter the donors by telling them what they wanted to hear turned donor meetings in Addis Ababa into daggers-drawn exercises. In November 1983, Libby Grimshaw of Save the Children said of that month's conference: 'The unpleasantness at the meeting came from questions from various embassies about the reality of requests from the RRC, about the amount of grain in the stores, about the closure of Assab, the incapacity of RRC transport and organization, the priorities of the Government and so on.' Dawit's disinterest in mollifying the donors could have had some impact on their preparedness to help. In particular he revelled in an antagonistic relationship with the Americans, and rarely let an intervention from the American Chargé d'Affaires go by without a contemptuous reference to 'Comrade Ambassador ...'

In some of this, Dawit was giving expression to Ethiopian

characteristics that I find admirable. Like the British whom they are said in many ways to resemble, the Ethiopians are an island race. Their highlands are their island, surrounded by the lowlands and the desert. Ethiopians regard themselves as African in just the way that the British regard themselves as European – that is, with qualifications. Marxist though their leadership may have been for a decade or so, the Ethiopians are the possessors of a glorious cultural heritage. And any prickly reserve may spring from the number of times they have been attacked and have repulsed those attacks. With the exception of Mussolini's brief occupation when the international community again failed to come to Ethiopia's aid, the country has remained independent. During the imperial carve-up of Africa in the nineteenth century, Ethiopian forces under the Emperor Menelik II annihilated the Italians at the battle of Adwa in the only defeat inflicted on a European army in Africa that century. Prickliness may result from national pride wounded by the famine conditions which have forced the Ethiopians to go abroad to beg.

Before the RRC was established, there was no effective mechanism for bringing assistance to bear at times of famine, let alone for raising international alarms. A medieval Ethiopian proverb still has currency: 'God cannot be blamed and the Emperor cannot be accused.' In his fine study of famine in modern Ethiopia* Professor Mesfin Wolde Mariam traces the official response to starvation in one area of Wollo in 1965. The matter was first reported by the local police station; a month later the Ministry of the Interior responded by asking for clarification; after seven *months* the Ministry of Interior was asking again for clarification; the local police was able to report back immediately that people were now leaving their homes *en masse*; six weeks later, they requested food; a fortnight passed and the local police put the famine death toll in the area at 2,738; this time the news reached the Emperor himself after only three weeks, and by then there were other reports arriving in Addis Ababa; as a final bureaucratic shot intended to discourage such enthusiastic reporting in future, the Ministry of Interior asked the police station in Wollo to send along the names of the dead. It would hardly be surprising if such official indifference had not sustained an attitude of fatalism.

Professor Mesfin, who was chairman of the inquiry into the last

* Mesfin Wolde Mariam; *Rural Vulnerability to Famine in Ethiopia: 1958–77*, Vikas Publishing House, Delhi.

great famine, discovered in Government files a circular letter sent to district authorities in Wollo during 1973 which instructed local administrators to assemble and pray for mercy every day, 'since there is no other solution except repentance and prayer'. Fatalism runs deep in the Ethiopian character. Professor Mesfin speaks of whole families in rural areas simply shutting their doors on famine and dying in stoic silence. Such attitudes persist among some surprising people. After our filming in Korem in 1984, we flew back to Addis Ababa in a chartered aircraft. I told the pilot what we had witnessed and filmed. He was very troubled, and then looked up from his controls to tell me that Ethiopians were being punished by God for their sins.

The establishment of the RRC was intended to change this. The centrepiece of its operation would be an early-warning system so that fears about future famines could be given concrete and scientific shape. This would enable donors to respond in time to future emergencies. In the early years of the revolutionary Government, the United States and Britain joined UNICEF, the United Nations Children's Fund, in financing the new system. But what the rich world gives, the rich world can also take away. And with the virtual closure of British and American development programmes in Ethiopia in 1979, funding provided to the RRC by the British Overseas Development Administration and the United States Agency for International Development also came to a halt. The early-warning system has continued to function with considerable efficiency with the assistance of UNICEF, but with the removal of Western support its deficiencies can hardly be blamed on the Ethiopians. There is a more profound irony here. The early warning functions of the RRC are the creation of Western aid donors who, if they are to provide help, demand modern scientific approaches to old problems. When the early-warning system signalled disaster in the early months of 1984, the Western aid donors were not listening.

As famine conditions built up in the countryside, UNICEF sponsored a special conference on the workings of the early-warning system. All sorts of clever things were said at this conference about how the system could be improved. In its crop assessments, the RRC can already call upon the services of Government evaluators who travel to the districts to interview Government administrators, peasant associations and local Ministry of Agriculture officials about what is happening to the crops. The RRC also has authority to utilize

35

information and personnel from the Government Meteorological Office and from the Ministry of Agriculture in making its analysis. Of course there are improvements that can be made. Like the RRC itself, its early-warning service is critically short of funds, short of transport and short of properly trained field personnel. I have visited RRC offices in the field that have no telephones, no files and no vehicles, just a man with a notebook trying to keep abreast of a raging famine.

One speaker at the August conference called for earlier reports to donors, but would they have made the slightest difference in 1984? An American Embassy representative suggested 'a series of regular meetings between the RRC and the donor agencies', but this was at a time when the world's biggest food aid provider was committing pathetically little to Ethiopia and had never yet been happy to commit aid through the RRC.

With what I take to be a certain exasperation, Mr Taye Gurmu, deputy commissioner of the Relief and Rehabilitation Commission, reminded the conference that the early warning system was not an end in itself. 'There is a clearly defined objective in the production of its figures and reports,' he said, 'and that objective is action on behalf of those affected by food shortages. If action does not result, there is little point in the system itself.' The failure of the aid-givers to take the RRC's famine warnings seriously was allied to another failure that cost Ethiopia dear in 1984: resistance to the idea of food stockpiles in Ethiopia.

Plans for a Food Security Reserve in Ethiopia are as old as the last big famine. They make a lot of sense. Instead of relying during every crisis on mobilizing a distracted world community, the RRC would have food ready to distribute. The idea was first canvassed in 1975 and then commended by the Food and Agricultural Organization of the United Nations in 1979. The initial stockpile would be 60,000 tonnes, rising to 120,000 tonnes. The United Nations would contribute the first 12,000 tonnes, and monitor the build-up of the stockpile for the first four years, by which time, the UN said, 'the full grain reserve should be established'. If the plan had been carried out, there would have been 120,000 tonnes of grain on hand – much more than was committed by donors to Ethiopia during the first nine months of 1984 – to check the worst effects of the famine. But it was an aid pipe-dream.

The United Nations was as good as its word. Their 12,000 tonnes were delivered into Ethiopia's new food reserve in 1982, and the RRC waited for the rest to bring the total up to twelve times that figure. It never came. Three years later the Dutch Government contributed 5,000 tonnes and that was the lot. By then, Ethiopia was in desperate need of emergency supplies, and the notion of a food reserve was redundant. But the refusal to consider it earlier remains difficult to fathom. 'Donors find themselves obliged at the end of the day to help,' says Commissioner Dawit, 'so why not contribute in good time to a proper reserve fund? If we had had such a reserve in 1984, we could have prevented much loss of life.'

The two donors that could reasonably have been expected to contribute to such a reserve were the United States and the European Community. Both have massive surpluses. As we shall see, the United States was so deeply antagonistic towards the Ethiopian régime that she disqualified herself from making any such gesture. The European Commission on the other hand is proud of its aid relationship with Ethiopia and could well have contributed. Some say that the reluctance of the grain-surplus donors to contribute to food reserves is because they may have an undesirably stabilizing impact on the world grain market, but I suspect that the real reason is more prosaic, and has more to do with the hand-to-mouth food aid relationship that a system of annual budgets encourages.

The reluctance of the rich countries to respond to the appeals of Ethiopia's Relief Commission is the less easy to understand because the Commission enjoys a remarkably high reputation among the aid agencies. The United States Government, for instance, has gone out of its ways to publicize its criticisms of the Ethiopian régime for failing to give a high enough priority to the famine, but the RRC won a grudging commendation. Through clenched teeth, the State Department acknowledged that aid donors considered the RRC to be a 'relatively well-organized and well-run organization'.

In its internal evaluation of the famine response that I have already quoted, Oxfam stated that the RRC's record 'cannot be heavily criticized', and went on to say that weaknesses in its early-warning system 'appear to be due to lack of funding, but were in any case not so great as to discredit the entire system'. A UNICEF official in Addis Ababa went on the record to say that Ethiopa had 'one of the best early-warning systems in the world', and Michael Harris, who in 1984 was Oxfam's immensely experienced Overseas Director, described the RRC as 'infinitely better than corresponding organizations in many other countries'.

This reputation should have counted for something when, some weeks after launching the March appeal, Commissioner Dawit set off on a tour of the major donors to place further emphasis on Ethiopia's needs. At the United Nations in New York he declared: 'Unless the situation is salvaged, and salvaged immediately, through a generous and concerted action by the international community, the widespread fears and dire warnings that the death toll may rise to truly catastrophic proportions may well come to pass.' So strained were relations with the United States that the Ethiopians calculated that meetings with American officials were not worth even requesting. From New York, Dawit travelled to Canada, the United Kingdom, the European Commission headquarters in Brussels, and to Italy. There was a response from Canada and a response of sorts from Brussels that we will be examining later, but for the rest Dawit returned empty-handed. 'They all said they would consider the situation very seriously,' he told me. 'But when I got back, I found I had achieved nothing. There were no new pledges.'

Ethiopia's relations with Britain were only marginally warmer than those with the United States. Towards the end of 1983, Dawit had had a disagreeable first meeting with Timothy Raison, the Overseas Development Minister, during which he was presented with the details of recent British press allegations that food aid to the RRC had been misappropriated by the army. 'He was very critical of all our activities,' Dawit recalled. 'I told him that we might have made mistakes, but that the RRC was one of the most effective organizations of its sort in Africa, and that I had come to get help.'

When Dawit arrived in London in May 1984, he was seen in Raison's absence by Malcolm Rifkind, Minister of State at the Foreign Office. The Commissioner spelt out out in some detail the extent of the food crisis that Ethiopia was currently facing. Rifkind was able to respond by saying that the British intended to give £300,000 to a number of voluntary agencies for use in Ethiopia. It was a modest sum, and also reflected a dubious tactic adopted by the Overseas Development Administration under the Conservatives. The ODA has doubled its contributions to private charities, and while it is true that these agencies get more for their money than do official agencies, such grants enable the British Government to maintain a high profile by helping bodies in the public eye at very small cost. Dawit was to be disappointed if he expected a British response to his larger food aid shopping list. 'I was told that the British were not going to do anything for 1984, but they would look at requests for 1985,' he told me.

The overall response to the March appeal could scarcely have been less generous. Ethiopia was in fact likely to get less in 1984 that in previous years. Canada, the European Commission and the World Food Programme promised to send grain; so too did the Soviet Union. The Russians were to be roundly abused later in the year for their lack of generosity by both the Americans and the British, who at this juncture pledged nothing. The Russians promised 10,000 tonnes of rice, and others in the Communist bloc made a gesture as well. The North Koreans and the Chinese came up with around 6,000 tonnes of grain, and the Cubans said they would send 5,000 tonnes of sugar. It was hardly magnificent solidarity, but it was something.

Just as bad as the paucity of the response was its extraordinary slowness. Five months after the March appeal for 450,000 tonnes, the RRC reported that 87,000 tonnes of grain and 8,000 tonnes of other food had been pledged, but that 'no shipment of the pledged food commodities has yet been received in our stores'. Widespread deaths from starvation were now being recorded in Wollo, and the RRC had run out of grain to distribute in the middle of July. 'In the light of the general crippling nature of the drought throughout the country and the further depletion of the country's known food grain sources,' said the RRC in a deadpan statement in August, 'one can simply note the consequences that may follow in the near future.' But apparent coolness concealed, according to one senior official, a sense of mounting panic in the RRC. That panic turned to anger when donor representatives next assembled at the Ghion Hotel in early October to hear once again from Commissioner Dawit.

Never a respecter of Western claims to put humanity above politics, Dawit was at his most abrasive. 'We will never be able to have an accurate estimate of the lives lost and the number of malnourished persons and displaced people caused by the irresponsible and indifferent attitude of certain Governments and organizations who had the capacity to do better,' he told his listeners. 'The fact that Ethiopia has chosen the path of socialism has made it a pariah in the view of some.' It was not lack of information, or lack of public concern in the West. 'It could never be anything else except sheer apathy, or the politicization of humanitarian aid,' he said. Dawit referred to Western complaints of aid going astray as distortions intended 'to justify an embargo on humanitarian aid'. As well as the lack of food aid, none of the transport or other requests had been met. 'What I find to be also beyond belief, appalling and even more pathetic, is the tendency in some corners to stay on the sidelines watching, as though it were a show of human tragedy.'

In his *Decline and Fall of the Roman Empire*, Edward Gibbon wrote of the remoteness and antiquity of Ethiopian civilization: 'Encompassed on all sides by the enemies of their religion, the Ethiopians slept near a thousand years, forgetful of the world by whom they were forgotten.' It is a much quoted passage and may have informed the parallel that Commissioner Dawit drew in yet another hammering of the donors in December 1984. Looking back in anger at the shocking lack of response to the RRC's major appeal in March, he said: 'Ethiopia was being forgotten by a world glutted with a surplus of grain.'

4

An Unhelpful Mission

One of the by-products of public agitation in the West about the famine in Africa was the manufacture of some plausible myths by the politicians and administrators involved. It became, for a time, quite a cottage industry. At a conference entitled 'Africa: the road to recovery' held in London in July 1985, a questioner wondered whether the United Nations had really done all it might to alert the world to the impending crisis. On the platform were Bradford Morse, executive director of the UN Office for Emergency Operations in Africa, and Lord Ennals, chairman of the United Nations Association in Britain. Both were dumbfounded by the suggestion. Failed to alert the world? Why, the Secretary-General of the United Nations, the Director-General of the Food and Agriculture Organization, Mr Morse himself, as head of the UN Development Programme, had all frequently warned of disaster around the corner. It was not their fault they were ignored. Next to them on the platform was the Conservative MP Bowen Wells, who takes a close interest in aid matters, and he wanted to put the record straight just in case anyone might think that national Governments like the British had been slow to react. He assured his listeners that the problem lay in the fact that neither the Ethiopians nor the Sudanese had been keen to let the world know about their famines. Lord Ennals, who was chairing the meeting, thanked Mr Wells for his valuable intervention, and the conference moved on to discuss Africa's road to recovery.

Mr Wells had a point as regards the Sudan, as we shall see, but in the case of Ethiopia no one can possibly maintain that the British and other Governments were not begged to assist at a time when assistance could have saved tens of thousands, probably hundreds of thousands of lives. The role of the United Nations is more tangled, but it is a useful journalist's rule of thumb that institutions should be judged not by what they say in their press releases, but by what they do.

The UN's Food and Agriculture Organization – based in Rome – anticipated the queries and criticisms that might emerge on its role in the 1984 Ethiopian famine, and set out to stifle them. A paper prepared for the Foreign Affairs Committee of the British House of Commons spelt out the initiatives it took on an Africa-wide basis from the beginning of 1983; it then published a more detailed chronology that dealt with warnings and assessments on the food crisis in Ethiopia from December 1982.

After the scare the world received about declining food supplies in the early 1970s, the FAO was in a good position to monitor future crises. Its Global Information and Early Warning System, now run by an impressive American, Barbara Huddleston, was set up in 1975, and among other data uses the latest in satellite technology to predict trouble. The METEOSAT satellite of the European Space Agency provides information on cloud cover, and the American LANDSAT monitors vegetation patterns. 'If the vegetation is receding, then there's a drought,' says Ms Huddleston. 'Before we got ground information from Ethiopia, we had been able to pick up all the signs of dryness.'

The FAO began ringing the alarm bells from early in 1983, but it was ringing them on behalf of no fewer than twenty-two African countries. Thus, in a telegram to donors sent in May 1983, Edouard Saouma, the Lebanese who runs the FAO, said: 'I am hopeful that you will generously respond to my appeal for increased assistance to these really needy countries.' Later in the year, Saouma referred to 150 million people in twenty-two countries facing distress 'which may reach proportions of hunger and malnourishment on a massive scale'. It was not until very much later in 1984, indeed not until after television had begun to take a close interest in the extent of starvation in Ethiopia, that the FAO began to demonstrate particular anxiety for that country. It did not even mention Sudan at that point.

The FAO's list of what Rome described at one juncture as 'calamity-affected' countries ran to twenty-four in 1984, slipping back to twenty-one in 1985. Since the calculations are based on crop years and because crop years vary in different parts of Africa, the list rose at one stage to twenty-seven countries. It was almost certainly too long, and its length may have owed as much to diplomacy in Rome as desperate scarcity in Africa. The respect for national sensibilities that kept Sudan off the list for far too long may also have contributed to getting other countries onto the list for hand-outs. The result was that the impact of Saouma's appeals to the donor community was blunted, and the countries facing mass death by starvation were the losers. 'No particular effort was made to highlight Ethiopia,' a senior FAO official told me in Rome. 'It was just one of the twenty-four countries affected.'

The length of the FAO list came in for public criticism when the House of Commons Foreign Affairs Committee took evidence in late 1984. 'FAO lost quite a lot of credibility this year because they have "cried wolf" a very great deal, and more or less made out that the whole of Africa is suffering from a food shortage, which is not true,' Michael Harris, Oxfam's Overseas Director, told the committee. 'They have spread a lot of alarm and despondency. If they had not done this quite so much, we could have concentrated a bit more on areas that did suffer.'

Different organizations have drawn up their own 'shortlists' of the worst-affected countries. The European Commission identified eight, the Commons Foreign Affairs Committee numbered nine, and by mid-1985 the FAO itself was concentrating on the few worst-off. Of the twenty-one countries still on its list, the FAO said that 'particular attention needs to be focused on the immediate requirements of the six most affected countries: Chad, Ethiopia, Mali, Mozambique, Niger and Sudan.' These six accounted for two-thirds of total food aid needs in Africa and for more than half of all undelivered food aid commitments. But diplomacy still exercised its grip at the UN. When a special conference was held in Geneva in March 1985, there were twenty African countries represented. The Economist Development Report commented that twelve of the twenty African countries should have been left off the list and outside the conference. 'But political pressures intervened,' it said.

The FAO made one key initiative in emphasizing the problems faced by Ethiopia. Along with its Rome-based associate the World Food Programme, the FAO dispatched a special mission from its Office for Special Relief Operations in February 1984. The mission spent a month in Ethiopia and was thus working closely with the Relief and Rehabilitation Commission as it prepared its own appeal for the end of March. The four-man mission had as its brief 'to evaluate the food supply situation and the logistic problems related to the mobilization of food within Ethiopia'. Had it endorsed the RRC's own view of the emergency and the response needed, the mission could

43

have had a vital impact on the urgency with which the donor community responded. Instead the report was an extraordinary curate's egg which seemed to endorse all the RRC's workings, but to. shrink from its conclusion.

To judge how negative was the impact of the FAO mission, it is important to recall the RRC's view of Ethiopia's needs. The RRC calculated that the country needed some 900,000 tonnes of grain to avert starvation during 1984, but in appreciation of its transport problems and possibly in acknowledgement of security difficulties, the RRC pitched their appeal at half their requirements, 450,000 tonnes. In one of the more fateful conclusions made by any set of experts in the build-up to the Ethiopian famine, the FAO mission slashed that figure by almost three-quarters. Thus after two bureaucracies, one local and one international, had had their say, national needs of 900,000 tonnes emerged as a UN-backed appeal for 125,000 tonnes.

Fortunately for the reputation of United Nations personnel, this conclusion was not allowed to go entirely unchallenged. Ten years before, at the time of the last great Ethiopian famine, it was a young UNICEF officer called Stephen Green who decided to break ranks and help the press tell the story of the 'unknown famine'. In 1984, the man who spoke up was the most senior UN official in Addis Ababa, Dr Kenneth King.

Dr King has a distinguished record of service both to the United Nations and to his home country, Guyana. He was for three years Guyana's Minister for Economic Development and was subsequently deputy to Edouard Saouma, Director-General of the FAO in Rome. As Resident Representative of the United Nations Development Programme in Addis Ababa, he was in 1984 one of the longest-serving UN officials in the country. The post of resident representative of UNDP also supposedly conferred additional responsibility upon him. It made him *ex officio* UN co-ordinator – in other words, the key official in the UN system in the event of a crisis like a famine. He was also representative in Addis Abba of the United Nations Disaster Relief Co-ordinator, the office established in the early 1970s to assume the co-ordinating role in the UN's response to disaster, and he was local head of the World Food Programme. It was a clutch of titles and responsibilities that one would have thought might guarantee Dr King a decisive say when a mission of non-resident experts blew into town. Sadly for Ethiopia it did no such thing.

For Dr King, the first mistake had already been made by the RRC. It should not have allowed itself arbitrarily to cut its needs in half because of its distribution problems. 'I don't think any of the actors came out of this particularly well,' Dr King told me later. But it was the further massive reduction of 325,000 tonnes by the UN for which Dr King reserved most of his anger. He argued the case strenuously with members of the mission and with colleagues in the local offices of the Food and Agriculture Organization and the World Food Programme, but lost. He then went public in his criticisms.

In May 1984, he was interviewed for a British Independent Television documentary 'Seeds of Despair', which was screened in July and was the first media alert to the growing tragedy in Ethiopia. Dr King was withering in his condemnation of the UN's own conduct which he described as 'an exercise in cynicism. People who do not agree with me say that they're being realistic. But it does appear to me that in 1984, with all the resources of the world, it should be possible to overcome at least some of the obstacles to getting the food into the country. And I'm not talking only figures, what we're talking about are lives. One hundred and twenty-five thousand tons would be a seventh, 14 per cent, which means that we're condemning by a stroke of the pen 86 per cent of the people who are affected to, if not death, then to a sort of half life, to a life without food over long periods. This I cannot accept.' It was a devastating statement and, in the light of subsequent reaction to the Ethiopian famine, a permanent reproach to leading United Nations agencies.

Dr King's interview was not well received at the headquarters of the United Nations Development Programme in New York, although their main concern was not his observations about how the UN was letting people starve in Ethiopia. In the same programme he had been asked about Ethiopia's development needs and why neither the United States nor Britain saw fit to give the country any development assistance. 'I think it's to do with the fact that Ethiopia has embraced the socialist philosophy,' he replied, adding a muted reference to superpower rivalry, 'and that one of Ethiopia's allies is not an ally of the British and Americans.' It could scarcely have been a less exceptional observation, but it merited a rap on the knuckles for Dr King in New York, because 'the donors did not like it', a reference to the United States Government which is a major contributor to the UNDP.

For reasons that are still not clear, the FAO/WFP mission report was not published until June, more than three months after the mission had left Addis Ababa. It is thirty pages or so in length, and cannot have taken too long to prepare. When an important report containing a UN-backed appeal is published, it is often the practice at FAO headquarters in Rome to devote a special donors' meeting to the subject. On this occasion, no such meeting was convened. Instead the Director-General of the FAO sent a telex to donors stating that Ethiopia's 'consumption deficit' was almost 600,000 tonnes, in itself a major reduction in what the RRC was estimating, but emphasizing that Ethiopia's distribution capacity was limited to 125,000 tonnes.

Probably the most damaging aspect of the mission's work was that it governed the outlook of both UN headquarters staff in Rome and field staff in Addis Ababa for much of the rest of the year. As early as March 1984, when the curious UN consensus that logistics should govern food needs was emerging, the World Food Programme was issuing one of its early reports on food aid deliveries to Africa. Ethiopia's needs on this occasion were put at 300,000 tonnes (in the early months of the emergency, figures have a habit of being plucked out of mid-air) but the report also recorded that aid donors had already pledged 176,000 tonnes, that the Relief Commission was holding some 45,000 tonnes in the North, and that the Government's grain-purchasing agency had 'carry-over stocks of 240,000 tonnes of cereals, mostly in the southern and western parts of the country which have benefited from reasonable harvests and face storage problems'. There were said to be problems of inadequate port capacity for shifting larger quantities of grain, a lack of vehicles and storage in the drought areas, and poor roads. As Oxfam's internal evaluation commented: 'There could hardly have been a clearer way of saying that there was no need for further food aid.'

There is little doubt that assessments like this from Rome provided Governments in the West with the means to challenge more alarming reports of deterioration in Ethiopia. As late as August, for instance, the World Food Programme was suggesting that the gap between food aid requirements and food aid commitments for 1984 was a manageable 50,000 tonnes. Officials of the British Overseas Development Administration claim that they were given the impression by the FAO in the middle of 1984 that 'there was enough grain in the country', and they used this argument to fend off criticism from the Commons Foreign Affairs Committee that the Government had been slow to respond to the emergency. 'In July 1984, the prospects for the main crop of cereals in Ethiopia were described as "favourable",' said the ODA.

In the field, the voluntary agencies had tended to rely upon their big brothers in the UN system for judgements and expertise in such technical areas as crop assessment. After the experience of 1984 in Ethiopia, they will be rather less inclined to do so in future. In May 1984, Oxfam headquarters told their Ethiopian field director Hugh Goyder of alarming Red Cross reports that spoke of a food emergency of 'crisis proportion'. Goyder's response from Addis Ababa was to quote the experts: 'WFP's basic contention, which I cannot question at this point, is that local stocks of domestically produced grain are adequate to meet both normal consumption requirements and the extra requirements of the drought ...' It was a conclusion that he was bitterly to regret.

In Oxfam's internal analysis of what went wrong, Hugh Goyder commented, 'I will never forgive myself for believing, back in May 1984, that WFP or FAO knew something about Ethiopia's food aid needs.' He said that the voluntary agencies in Ethiopia, including Oxfam, had gone through a 'learning curve' during the summer of 1984. 'We tended to believe their figures until about June when the gravity of the food deficits became all too clear. By September, the WFP's poor presentation of food aid statistics at CRDA [Christian Relief Development Association] meetings was greeted with ridicule by many present.' It is fair to say that in its food aid monitoring role later in the famine crisis, the World Food Programme emerged as one of the relatively few bureaucratic success stories, but by then a lot of Ethiopians were dead.

What went wrong in 1984? The UN mission's key error – more abundantly plain in retrospect than it may have been at the time – was to underestimate the capacity of the creaky Ethiopian port and distribution system to get food moving in a crisis. It was reckoned for instance that Ethiopia's principal port, Assab, could handle a maximum of 1,200 tonnes a day. Yet when the grain began arriving in quantity at the end of the year, Assab sustained an off-take of at least 3,000 tonnes a day. The result was that in a year of stepped-up efforts by the international community, Assab and other ports were able to handle more than the 900,000 tonnes first specified by the RRC as the country's needs. 'We never believed it was possible to bring in one

47

million tonnes in a year,' a member of the UN mission told me later in Rome.

As far As Dr King is concerned, the error was one of approach. The priority should have been to meet Ethiopia's humanitarian needs. 'Surely if you have a problem, you don't say "I can't find the solution" when there are lives at stake,' he told me. 'You must intensify the pressure until the solution is found. If you're going to err, you must err – shall I say it – on the side of humanity.'

The next mistake made by the UN was over stocks of grain already in the country, although here the blame seems to be shared with Ethiopia's Agricultural Marketing Corporation (AMC). The AMC is a monument to socialist planning. Its role is to buy from farmers at prices that provide little incentive to producers, and then to sell to those favoured by the administration. That means the AMC sells to Government institutions such as the army and the militia – Ethiopia's embattled forces march on their stomachs, too – and what is left goes to the city dwellers. The cities must be kept tolerably happy because in Ethiopia, as elsewhere, it is the cities not the countryside that present a possible challenge to the Government. If the régime needed a reminder of these priorities, the course of 1974's 'creeping coup' was clear enough. Haile Selassie's imperial régime might have survived prolonged starvation in the countryside; when food shortages and price rises spread to Addis Ababa and the demonstrations began, his days were numbered.

It is certain that executives of the Agricultural Marketing Corporation provided the UN with an overly rosy account of their stock position in February 1984. Members of the visiting mission from Rome say they were told that the AMC actually had a storage problem and that it had been selling grain at well below market prices in Addis Ababa simply to get rid of it. Figures around 200,000 tonnes were mentioned and duly recorded in the mission's report. The head of the AMC was reported in 1985 to have paid the price for this optimism by being moved from his post.

But what is equally certain is that this grain was never available for free relief, a fact also carefully recorded in the mission's report. 'The Government lacks the budgetary resources to finance the transfer of grains from the AMC to the RRC,' the report said. 'Therefore, financial support would be necessary to purchase these grains if they are to be used to meet the supply problem in the northern regions.' It was a crucial distinction because the Government would never give away food supplies earmarked for its important clients in the administration and the cities. Indeed, an emergency hand-over of some 60,000 tonnes of grain from the AMC to the RRC to plug a yawning supply gap had to be paid back later in the year when international relief aid began at last to arrive. The problem was that this key distinction was not properly made until the mission's report was published in June and, in the meantime, the World Food Programme in the field had put forward its fateful estimate of the amount of grain available in Ethiopia. There was also little chance that the eventual publication of the report would correct many misapprehensions. In the name of confidentiality, the FAO issues such reports neither to the press, which may be understandable, nor to the voluntary agencies, which is unforgivable.

The issue of Ethiopia's supposedly massive grain reserve should have been sorted out by June 1984 at the latest. By then, it is now conceded by the FAO, the cupboard was bare, although the World Food Programme continued to insist for some while that the deficit was not disastrous. There was nothing sinister in the run-down of AMC stocks; the agency was simply fulfilling its role of keeping important people in the administration and the cities fed. Among the first outsiders to note the enormity of the food gap were Canadian government officials. They too had been sceptical of RRC claims at the beginning of the year, but they began to change their tune in June. Privately, they were even challenging the notion that the Government had ever had particularly healthy food stocks. They argued that anticipated surpluses had never materialized because of poor harvests on the State farms at the end of 1983, and because small farmers were not selling their produce to the Government in 1984.

Members of the UN mission acknowledge that they simply failed to detect what a serious situation was building up in the northern provinces. 'Security problems' prevented them from even getting to Wollo, epicentre of famine deaths later in the year. 'We failed to understand the cumulative effects of problems in the North,' one member of the mission admitted to me in Rome. 'People's reserves – in grain as well as in their own physical strength – had become progressively reduced so that a small factor would bring them to catastrophe.'

A senior official responsible for the preparation of the FAO's early-warning information added: 'We simply did not anticipate the gravity of the situation. We believed that there were greater surpluses in the south, and we anticipated more of a northwards movement of grain. We thought there would be hardship, but not a famine.' This explanation, honest and forthright as far as it goes, ignores what the mission was being told in Ethiopia. RRC officials emphasized, for instance, that reserves held by the Agricultural Marketing Corporation could not be used for relief, and Berhane Gizaw, head of early warning and statistics, recalled an exchange with members of the mission in which he tried to convince them that peasants in the North had sold all their livestock and their possessions and that they had nothing left.

A member of the mission replied: 'You have been telling the world of this problem in 1982 and 1983, but we've not seen the people dying like flies yet.' It was not the most attractive face of the FAO.

Scepticism over a Government's view of its own needs is perhaps quite proper for the UN. In the case of Ethiopia, there may even be a justified complaint about Government secrecy and its persistent failure to account in detail for the use of its food stocks, domestic or donated. A tradition of independence, allied to a fear of the consequences of Western hostility, may account for Ethiopian reluctance to open all its books for scrutiny. But that in itself does not excuse the UN. Their failure to come up with an adequate assessment of Ethiopia's needs had a substantial effect on the progress of the famine. It also affected the UN's relationship with the Ethiopians. 'There was a breakdown of trust between the UN and the RRC after March,' recalled Hugh Goyder of Oxfam. 'Mutual confidence had been lost.'

Dr King sustained the criticism that began at the time of the joint FAO/WFP mission. 'They talked to FAO experts and the Ethiopian Government's Central Statistical Office,' he told me. 'Then they chose figures that FAO men in the field didn't accept. Their figures were unsubstantiated.' He believed they may have been too influenced by views of Ethiopian endeavours encountered on the diplomatic circuit. 'They chose "cocktail" figures,' he added dismissively. Dr King also argued that what happened in Ethiopia in 1984 was part of a more pernicious trend. 'The UN is supposed to be an objective body,' he said. 'But it's become far too donor-oriented. Some say we have to be.

But that's not good enough. You've got to follow your own convictions.'

By early 1985, Rome's reporting system had improved out of all recognition. Indeed, the World Food Programme had become central to the logistics operation throughout the famine-affected areas of Africa. By then all the right distinctions were being made between food that had been committed and food that had arrived, and between food that was for emergency use and free food for development projects. But in the critical early months in Ethiopia information from Rome was misleading. In July, the FAO was reporting that 230,000 tonnes of food had either been received or was in the pipeline to Ethiopia. On 6 August, the RRC reported that it had received only 34,000 tonnes of relief grain since its March appeal. Faced with such contradictions, the world tended to believe the UN agencies, and the world was wrong. Between March and October 1984, the Oxfam famine study stated, the international failure to respond to the Ethiopian famine 'may to some extent be attributed to the misleading reports of the World Food Programme'.

At the end of 1984, another mission was despatched from Rome to Addis Ababa. This one was to assess the year's crops. It concluded that Ethiopia's production would be between 25 and 30 per cent below normal, leading to a grain shortfall of between 1.7 million and 2 million tonnes. In the overwhelming statistics of Ethiopia's famine, the mission added: 'This may be roughly equivalent to the ordinary consumption of between 6.5 to 8 million people.' It was late in the day for such an acknowledgement, but it may have given RRC officials some satisfaction to be able to record in their December report to donors that 'at last the assessment of these organizations regarding the gravity of the drought and famine situation was approaching the assessment of the RRC'.

5

'A Hungry Child Has No Politics'

Senator John Danforth's slide show is credited with having obtained $90 million from President Reagan for the African famine emergency. In January 1984, the Republican Senator from Missouri toured eight African countries in two weeks, returned to Washington in the middle of a blizzard, and sent his photographs straight off to be processed. The same afternoon he had an appointment with the President and showed him the pictures. 'I can say he was really moved by them,' the Senator said. 'This is not some professional photographer; this is just me pointing my camera,' said Danforth when he repeated the performance in March for colleagues on the Senate Foreign Relations Committee. But the Subcommittee on African Affairs ordered them to be printed, and Senator Danforth's pictures now form part of the Congressional record. Most of them are from Mozambique – he did not· visit Ethiopia – which was then undergoing a severe famine exacerbated like Ethiopia's by guerrilla activity against the Government. The first picture shows the United States Ambassador to Mozambique standing self-consciously in a dried-up field of corn; the others portray the results of those failed crops: children with distended bellies, children with empty bowls, children crying, children too ill to stand, children on the point of death from malnutrition – images of Africa that were to become commonplace later in the year. They had an effect then. The President ordered the addition of $90 million to the agreed 1984 foreign assistance budget. It would buy 225,000 tonnes of food, but it would not be enough.

For three decades and more, the United States has taken great pride in its capacity to respond to food emergencies around the world. The country's super-abundance in food sustains the world's largest surpluses, and it is calculated to be to everyone's advantage – farmer, administrator, foreign policy strategist as well as recipient – that the world's hungry should be fed. An informal target has been adopted by

American food aid administrators: that the United States would answer for half the world's food needs and the other donors could club together to meet the rest. It is a commitment that has regularly been honoured.

It was President Eisenhower who signed the Food-for-Peace programme into existence. For a generation, this programme, better known by its more prosaic title of Public Law, or simply PL 480, has been a constant in American relations with the Third World. The clasped hands of friendship and the legend 'Gift of the People of the United States of America' stamped on sacks of grain were symbols of US economic power, of US capacity to help its friends, and of US generosity. When Henry Kissinger declared his 'bold objective' in Rome in 1974 that within a decade no child would go to bed hungry, it was the United States (under a Republican Administration, at that) that would be spearheading the effort.

On 10 July 1984, the thirtieth anniversary of the food-for-peace programme, President Reagan launched what his press spokesman described as a 'major initiative' on the food aid front. It would allow the US 'to respond more quickly and effectively to the food needs of the people of Africa and the world suffering from hunger and malnutrition'. Among the measures to be taken was the pre-positioning of food stocks to reduce the response time to emergency from a few months to a few weeks. This had long been a dream of the UN's food planners. The President was also saying that internal transport costs should be borne under emergency feeding programmes, and there would be a 'business leaders' group' formed to examine Third World food problems.

Much of this was window-dressing. Internal transport costs were already being increasingly borne by the US and other aid-givers as a response to the virtual bankruptcy of many African recipients. Little was done to pre-position food stocks in Africa. Confronted by the full force of the famine emergency in 1985, American aid officials decided to pump huge quantities of grain into African ports. But the resultant stockpiles were much more to do with inadequate logistics in the African interior than the intelligent pre-positioning of supplies.

Once the American public had roused its Government into a response to the Ethiopian catastrophe, spokesmen for the Administration could plausibly claim that they had shouldered the customary burden. Well over one million tonnes of American relief food would

53

be delivered to Africa during 1985, and President Reagan had declared that he wanted $1 billion spent on the operation. About a third of the total would be fresh commitments. To Ethiopia alone the Americans were committing more than 300,000 tonnes. That represented about one-third of what the international community as a whole was delivering: some way off the traditional target of 50 per cent, but a tremendous quantity all the same. President Reagan was quoted as telling his chief aid administrator: 'McPherson, this is supposed to move, and we want to get it done, because we want to respond to those starving people.'

Aid to Ethiopia was to be strictly non-political. Administration spokesmen were emphatic about that. Peter McPherson, head of the United States Agency for International Development (USAID), set out America's no-strings-attached generosity in an article in the *Washington Post* in March 1985: 'The United States motto has been "A hungry child knows no politics." Our emergency aid will go anywhere there is hunger, regardless of our relationship with the Government in question. Ethiopia, where seven million are affected, is the largest recipient of our emergency aid to Africa despite the Marxist character of its Government.' The State Department publicly concurred with USAID. 'The United States has not allowed political differences with any Government to weaken its determination to have assistance reach those in need', it declared in April 1985. 'We are the largest donor to Ethiopia, a country whose Government had been openly hostile to us for several years.' At its folksiest, the same point was made by Millicent Fenwick, US Ambassador to the UN Food and Agricultural Organization in Rome. 'We don't care who's sitting in the palace when there's starvation in the street,' she said.

The central issue in US conduct towards the Ethiopian famine concerns what had happened before the explosion of public interest. Unlike other donors, the United States had an admitted capacity to bring substantial single-handed relief to the victims of famine in Ethiopia. In the two to three years of drought and bush-fire famines that led up to the holocaust of 1984, did the United States live up to Peter McPherson's ideal that 'A hungry child knows no politics'? Was that the rhetoric or the reality of the American response?

Congressman Howard Wolpe is a Michigan Democrat with a background in African affairs that finds acute expression in his chairmanship of the African Subcommittee of the House Foreign

Affairs Committee. He has lived and worked as a political scientist in Nigeria, and has taught African courses at university in his home state. With other members of his subcommittee he visited Ethiopia in August 1983, and thereafter harried officials over the United States response to the growing African emergency. His staff seem at times to have been running a crop evaluation service for the continent that rivalled and perhaps out-performed those of the United Nations and USAID.

Wolpe accepted in early 1985 that the United States had finally taken up its share of the burden. 'I think we can all be very proud of the response of the American people and the American Government in the past four months,' he told a House Appropriations Committee in February. Americans had seen the same BBC footage that galvanized Britain and Europe at the end of October 1984. 'But we also need to understand and face honestly the fact that had we responded over two years ago, when the basic facts were in about what was happening on the continent, literally tens of thousands of lives that had been lost could in fact have been saved.'

Because of the nature and progress of its revolutionary régime, Ethiopia disqualified itself on a number of grounds from US economic assistance. One amendment to the Foreign Assistance Act denied Ethiopia economic development help because the régime had not compensated all the United States interests nationalized after the revolution. Chief among them was the Kalamazoo Spice Co. of Michigan which had presented a $20 million claim for its Addis Ababa factory. Another amendment stopped economic assistance to Ethiopia because the country had not paid instalments on past loans for military assistance.

None of this should have affected American capacity to respond to recurrent famine in Ethiopia. Title 11 of PL 480 food assistance is intended specifically for relief purposes, and there were supposed to be no political barriers to its distribution. Such food is intended 'to meet famine or other urgent requirements, to combat malnutrition (especially in children) and to promote economic and community development'. Since 1982, one significant restriction had been placed on Title 11 emergency shipments to Ethiopia when USAID refused to channel food through the Government's Relief and Rehabilitation Commission. The restriction remained in place for two years. It was relaxed only when Peter McPherson of USAID reached a formal agreement with Commissioner Dawit of the RRC in Washington in November 1984 in the aftermath of massive television exposure of the famine in the United States. Ethiopia had to be declared a friendly country so that it could again receive direct government-to-government food assistance. But even when the restriction was in place, there was another avenue by which the United States could meet its obligations to provide emergency assistance – through American charities.

Like Save the Children Fund, Catholic Relief Services had been active in Ethiopia since the last great Ethiopian famine in the 1970s. With American relief food provided to them under Title 11 of the PL 480 programme, CRS had been running feeding centres for pre-school children and nursing mothers both in Addis Ababa and the big eastern town of Dire Dawa near the Somali border.

By late 1982, the Catholic Relief Services programme in Ethiopia was facing a crisis. Emergency needs were mounting in the country and yet Ethiopia was having its relief entitlement severely squeezed. Figures made available to Congress a year later confirmed the point. In 1980, Ethiopia received 43,000 tonnes of American food under the Title 11 programme; in 1981 that figure had been almost halved to 24,000 tonnes; in 1982 it was quartered again to 6,000 tonnes. The Ethiopian Government had already been cut out as a distributor, and the World Food Programme was now being phased out as well. CRS seemed to be hanging on only on temporary sufferance. According to the following year's budget proposals, running from October 1983, Ethiopia was to be removed entirely as a recipient of American humanitarian aid. USAID's noble maxim 'A hungry child knows no politics' was apparently inoperative.

The Christian soldiers of CRS pressed onward, however. Far from acknowledging that their regular programme for mothers and young children in Addis Ababa and Dire Dawa would have to close, or that they would have to look elsewhere for donors, CRS sought to get another project off the ground. At the time that Save the Children were starting their feeding centre in Korem, CRS looked 100 miles further north to Makelle, capital of the Tigre region and the other town where BBC Television cameras were to linger in October 1984. The Relief and Rehabilitation Commission had a feeding programme there for famine victims displaced from their homes in the countryside, but the equally hungry people of Makelle itself were getting nothing. Father Thomas Fitzpatrick, a Jesuit priest from Rochester, New York, who was the CRS field director in Ethiopia, called on the United States Embassy in December 1982 as the first step in his efforts to tackle the problem.

Senior personnel at the United States Embassy in Addis Ababa deferred to no one in their antipathy to the Ethiopian régime, but they had a respectable record during the famine years in forwarding, indeed recommending, proposals for emergency assistance. In framing his proposals for Makelle, Father Thomas ensured that they were both modest and precise. He asked for exactly 838 tonnes of food at a cost, including freight to an Ethiopian port, of $397,000. It would feed 5,000 families in the town for nine months, and CRS would pay for all transport costs within Ethiopia. Because it was an emergency, Father Thomas asked for permission to utilize US Title 11 stocks already held in the country by CRS. They could be returned when the 838 tonnes shipment arrived.

In a cable that was sent through the Embassy to Washington, Father Thomas dealt diplomatically with the security problem in Tigre, the only possible ground on which his scheme could be faulted. 'CRS/Ethiopia has decided to concentrate its activity on an emergency feeding programme in Makelle itself because this is one of the few places where commodities can be transported with some degree of security by moving in convoys from Assab and where such a programme can be carried out, given the limitations of travel in the area,' he stated. In justification of the programme, Father Thomas added: 'We are confident that given the desperate plight of the townspeople of Makelle, CRS/New York will be able to fund the minimal costs to bring to the people of Makelle this humanitarian assistance made possible by the people of the United States.' To this peroration was appended the endorsement 'Embassy supports this programme.'

Rarely can the United States Government have delayed so long to authorize so little. CRS received word that the 838 tonnes had been approved on 7 May 1983, five months after the request had reached Washington. According to spokesmen for USAID, such a proposal, particularly because it did not involve finding the money for internal transport, would normally be approved in between one and three weeks. The timing of the decision to authorize the shipment reflects equally little credit on the administrators of American aid. In early

May officials were informed that NBC had been given visas by the Ethiopian Government to film a drought story and that three national newspapers had submitted similar requests for visas.

Criticism of US conduct was duly forthcoming in a series of articles in the *Washington Post* in late June. Jay Ross, the *Post* Correspondent, asserted that the United States appeared 'to have bowed out of its customary role of providing relief because of Ethiopia's close ties to the Soviet Union'. He quoted Trevor Page, the energetic emergency officer of the World Food Programme, as saying: 'The US has taken the approach that it doesn't like the Ethiopian Government, so let some other countries bale out Ethiopia. But people who are in need of food don't care about Marxism or capitalism. They just have empty bellies that need to be filled.' The *Washington Post* pieces added to Congressional pressure on USAID to respond to emergency needs in Ethiopia. When CRS applied in July 1983 for 4,500 tonnes of food to expand the Makelle programme, the request was approved in nine days. The regular CRS mother-and-child programme was restored on 13 July. But that was not the end of the CRS battle to bring American charity to bear on the starving of Tigre.

A year after they had first identified the pressing needs of Makelle, CRS conducted a fresh survey in the area. Things did not look good. More than half the people at the feeding centre in the town were less than 80 per cent weight-for-height, in other words badly malnourished. In a rural programme run by the missionary Daughters of Charity, which CRS was supplying, three-quarters of the people were in a similar state. CRS also saw the need to expand into other towns in Tigre, and to start a programme further north in Eritrea.

On 13 October 1983, CRS applied to USAID for 16,000 tonnes of food. It would feed 35,000 families and an additional 14,000 destitutes in Tigre and Eritrea for nine months. A favourable response seemed likely. In August a USAID team had spent two weeks in Ethiopia and recommended an additional 15,000 tonnes of food. The same month, Representative Howard Wolpe led an eight-member Congressional mission to Ethiopia which concluded that thousands faced 'imminent death unless there is an immediate increase in the American and international relief assistance to Ethiopia'. Members of the delegation said that they would 'do everything he or she can to ensure an appropriate and prompt US Government response to the devastating food situation facing the people of Ethiopia'. CRS waited.

In December, two months after the request had been made, another USAID mission came to Ethiopia and recommended that the 16,000 tonnes should be approved immediately. CRS waited. In January, CRS in New York was told informally by USAID that they would be receiving 8,000 tonnes. In Ethiopia, CRS was forced to look for stop-gap sources of food to keep faith with the hungry of Tigre and Eritrea. First they diverted food from their regular mother-and-child feeding programme in the cities. For this, they needed and received authority from the US Embassy. Then they persuaded the Canadian Government to help with 5,000 tonnes of food shipped direct and another 2,000 tonnes through a Mennonite group. And still they waited for the US Government to honour its commitment to the 'Hungry child who knows no politics'. It is said that by now regional USAID officials in East Africa were becoming emotional in their cables to Washington: 'If you don't send this food, you're going to be responsible for the deaths of many children.' On 12 May 1984, USAID announced the approval of 8,000 tonnes of food, half the original request after a record delay of seven months. The authorization was so late and the Canadian stop-gaps so effective in Tigre and Eritrea that fresh authorization had to be sought from Washington to utilize the food elsewhere in the Ethiopian famine zones.

It was in the middle of this scandalous saga that Ken Hackett, regional director for Sub-Saharan Africa at CRS, testified to the House Subcommittee on African Affairs. It is worth recalling that he spoke a year before public horror at television pictures roused some insensible official consciences in the Western world. 'The drought of '83 will stretch into '84,' he said. 'Thousands will die. Somebody will count them. Somebody will survey the results of relief efforts. Most will criticize, but after all the papers have been published and books written, what will anybody learn? History teaches little to bureaucracy. But let's keep on trying.'

It is testimony to the American way of doing things that the story of the CRS requests has not remained under official wraps. In November 1984, when the extent of the Ethiopian disaster was at last appreciated, Congressman Byron Dorgan wrote to the United States General Accounting Office asking it to investigate the US response to the Ethiopian famine. The GAO reported in April 1985. The twenty-page report was remarkably buttoned-down in tone, but it was thorough and its conclusions were not reassuring.

The General Accounting Office report affirmed that 'the United States knew that a potentially serious food shortage situation existed in the northern provinces of Ethiopia in late 1982'. It stated that the 'initial US response was delayed because of strained relations between the two Governments and several policy and administrative concerns related to the provision of relief aid to Ethiopia'. As far as the two CRS requests were concerned, the report acknowledged that the scale of Ethiopia's needs and the small amounts involved 'raise legitimate questions as to the reasonableness of the delays'.

Some of the reasons advanced by officials for the slowness of the response are disingenuous at best, cynical excuses for inaction at worst. Much is made, for instance, of an ill-founded piece in the *Sunday Times* of London in March 1983 alleging that Western food aid to Ethiopia had been diverted to the Soviet Union to buy arms. We will be dealing in detail with the impact of this meagre piece of journalism on aid-giving attitudes in the next chapter, but it was eagerly seized upon in Washington. 'That set off an enormous amount of investigation,' said Julia Bloch, assistant administrator in charge of Africa for USAID. 'Later it was disproved. But that took time.'

Again, US officials pounced upon an Embassy report from Addis Ababa in November 1983 saying that tins of vegetable oil from a PL 480 emergency programme had been seen in local markets. 'I think it would be very irresponsible of us to move forward on the Ethiopian requests until we get to the bottom of the problems I have just mentioned,' Ms Bloch told a Congressional hearing in March 1984. All told, it took USAID officials six months to establish that the vegetable oil allegations were 'at the level of petty pilfering and resale of individual rations'.

None of this amounted to a solid reason for delay on the CRS requests. In the first place, no allegation had been made that any food supplied through CRS had gone astray. Secondly, USAID administrators were publicly emphatic that voluntary agencies were the best way of ensuring that food went to where it was intended. Ms Bloch herself testified before a Congressional hearing in November 1983: 'We believe that working with the voluntary agencies such as CRS gives us particular assurance that the food will get to those in need. The voluntary agencies have decades of experience in responding to emergency relief, and are equally concerned with getting food to the needy, quickly and effectively.' It was an ironic compliment to pay to an agency whose request for 16,000 tonnes of food was to be held up for another six months.

By the time political imperatives in Washington demanded urgent attention to Ethiopia's problems, allegations of food aid diversions were impatiently rejected. Richard Goldberg, a Deputy Under-Secretary at the Department of Agriculture, which played a principal role in vetting the CRS requests, was asked about evidence of diversion to the Ethiopian army at a Congressional hearing in February 1985. 'No,' he said. 'We are not aware of such diversion. The use of the private voluntary organizations in Ethiopia as a primary channel for US food aid greatly helps to ensure that the donated food reaches the intended recipient.' Peter McPherson, head of USAID, testified that emergency food aid was going well, 'because it is under the immediate guidance, care and control of Americans who are there or employees of Americans who are there with the food.' No such assurances had been accepted in the long months of waiting by CRS in 1983 and 1984.

The substantive grounds for withholding emergency food aid to Ethiopia were political. They can best be observed through what the Reagan Administration denied was an East-West prism. The General Accounting Office stated that the US Government needed to be assured 'that US-provided food was not being used either directly or indirectly to support a Government which is unfriendly to the United States'. Since USAID was apparently satisfied that there was no question of food supplied through Catholic Relief Services being hijacked by the Ethiopian Government for use by, say, the army, the problem was one of indirect support for the régime. By shipping relief supplies to Ethiopia, was the West propping up a Soviet-backed régime by enabling it to concentrate resources on the wars that kept it in power? The unwieldy term 'fungibility' was coined to describe this process and was much used by British civil servants in 1984–5 to account for their own lack of enthusiasm for any long-term commitment to Ethiopia.

For three years, the Ethiopian Government had made no commercial imports of grain. Was that because it did not recognize the crisis on its own doorstep? Or because it had no foreign exchange? Or because it was utilizing its precious foreign exchange to pay instalments to the Russians on a $2 billion arms bill? There was much debate on the matter within the Administration. The General

Accounting Office said in its report: 'Many officials within the US Government argued that donated food was saving foreign exchange for the Ethiopian Government and those savings increased its capacity to import military and non-essential goods and concentrate its funds on the war effort in the northern provinces. This concern remains open and is frequently debated, *but the US policy to feed hungry people is currently overriding that concern*' (my italics). The implications of this finding seem plain: that for a period in 1983 and 1984 humanitarian considerations and Peter McPherson's 'hungry child' were not paramount in Washington's view of the Ethiopian tragedy, and that with a further shift in US policy they could cease in future to be paramount.

Perhaps the most extraordinary aspect of the CRS requests was the procedure by which the decisions were taken in Washington. Almost everyone you could think of had a finger in the pie. It is a system that still apparently applies to the approval of emergency PL 480 Title 11 requests. In a controversial case like Ethiopia, it could almost have been designed to frustrate a humanitarian objective. As USAID administrator McPherson observed: 'When I first got here and saw the multiple voices, I thought, goodness, it just doesn't make good old American management sense.' But the system prevailed.

There is disagreement as to which Government agency chairs the authorizing committee. In evidence to a Senate hearing in September 1984, McPherson declared that it was the Department of Agriculture; in its report on the US response to the famine, the General Accounting Office stated that it was McPherson's own agency USAID. Some confusion also exists as to the role of such bodies as the US Treasury, the Department of Transportation and the Peace Corps in the decision-making, but there is no doubt that the key players are the Department of Agriculture, USAID, the State Department and the Office of Management and Budget. After USAID officials have examined the assistance request, senior officials representing these bodies meet and, according to the GAO, actually vote on who should be fed. Final approval is given only when a consensus emerges.

The General Accounting Office tried to examine in detail how the CRS requests were treated, but discovered virtually no documentation on them. They were unable to find out when the committee met to consider Ethiopia, how many times Ethiopian needs were discussed, what reasons were given for withholding authorization, or what views the different departments offered on the requests. What happened is thus a matter for speculation. It is safe to conclude that despite some of its public pronouncements USAID might have wanted the requests to be favourably received. The Department of Agriculture can have had no reasons of its own for stopping food going to Ethiopia. The State Department representative would doubtless have reflected the deep antagonism between the United States and Ethiopian Governments.

As its name implies, the Office of Management and Budget would have had a financial interest in the matter, but the sums involved were never large. The GAO report stated that the Office of Management and Budget also represented the National Security Council on the committee. This could have been the decisive influence. The National Security Council is one of the President's most senior policy advisory bodies, and helping Ethiopia might not have been a political priority. Whoever jammed the spoke in the wheel, the result was beyond speculation. For a total of twelve months, a quantity of less than 9,000 tonnes of emergency food aid had been withheld for political reasons from the hungry people of Ethiopia.

Before the GAO published its report in 1985, McPherson of USAID was called upon to defend the system of vetting requests before a Senate hearing. He acknowledged that there might sometimes be confusion, but added: 'It is my judgement that the system works better than what those who are not involved in it tend to think.' Senator Nancy Kassebaum, chairman of the African Subcommittee, tersely observed: 'I am sure it must.'

During 1984, the Reagan Administration had other opportunities to demonstrate how much of a priority it attached to famine in Africa. On 30 January, shortly after Senator Danforth's slide show for the President, the White House announced that it would seek a further $90 million from Congress for Africa. As soon as the announcement was made, it was clear that it would not be enough. USAID had already gone on record saying that it might not have enough money to meet food aid requests for the rest of the year, and even with the $90 million it would still be $14 million short. This was not even counting further emergency requests that might arrive in the course of the year.

Congress was already agitated by the decline in food aid to Africa during the Reagan years. From 1980 to 1983 its value had slipped from $186 million to $137 million. There had been testy exchanges on the subject at a Congressional hearing in November 1983 when Julia Bloch, head of the Africa Bureau at USAID, had tried to explain the figures away to Congressman Wolpe.

MR WOLPE: I don't think it is helpful to try to deny the reality of what has happened. The food aid programme, basic programme, has declined very sharply. Let me suggest that if you take not only dollar figures, but if you take, instead, tonnage figures ... the decline becomes even more precipitous.

MS BLOCH: Congressman, I take your point. I would say that we are trying to find ways to do more in sub-Sahara Africa in a way that addresses both the short-term and the long-term problems.

MR WOLPE: I appreciate that, but I think it is easier just to be a little bit free in acknowledging the empirical reality of what has happened.

It was hardly surprising, then, that Congress wanted to increase the $90 million which the Administration proposed to add to the annual $650 million foreign assistance budget. From the Senate, legislation was introduced to increase the figure to $150 million. Democrats in the House of Representatives went further. Ted Weiss, a colleague of Congressman Wolpe on the Africa Subcommittee, wanted a supplement of $300 million which, he argued, would enable the United States to meet its customary share of half of Africa's food needs. House Democrats had to wait until the next fiscal year for that sort of money to be committed.

In the early months of 1984, the key foreign policy issue on Capitol Hill was not the African famine at all, but Central America. And it was at this juncture that the two questions became entangled, to the disadvantage of hungry Africans. The Senate voted an additional $150 million for Africa on 6 March, but in committee two highly contentious Central American amendments were attached to it by Republican Senators at the prompting of the White House. One allowed for $93 million in military assistance to El Salvador, the other for $22 million in aid to the 'Contras' engaged in guerrilla warfare against the left-wing Government of Nicaragua.

The Administration's tactic – justified publicly on the grounds that it was the only way to get Central American military budgets through Congress – provoked outrage. Congressman Wolpe described the linkage as 'obscene', and with that familiar Irish-American rasp House Speaker 'Tip' O'Neill said that the Administration had 'shown it is ready to starve Africans so that it can kill Central Americans'.

Supporters of aid to Africa in the Senate had one counter-punch to throw. Senator Danforth, whose fireside slide show for the President may have accounted for the Administration's $90 million proposal in the first place, contrived to free the measure from its Central American swamp, re-attach it to an uncontentious piece of legislation about domestic heating subsidies, and get it through. Some two months after it was introduced, the $90 million supplemental was signed into law by President Reagan on 6 April. The remaining $60 million was still stuck fast in the swamp. Further deals had to be done. The House would have nothing to do with aiding the 'Contras', but was obliged to accept the link between military assistance to El Salvador and food aid to Africa. The measure was passed on that understanding and signed by the President on 2 July, four months after the Senate had voted for the extra $60 million. With only three months to run of the 1984 fiscal year, USAID was unable to spend the money. It was tossed into the far bigger pot available for combating famine in 1985.

USAID's appreciation of the mounting tragedy in Ethiopia had been patchy at best. Hampered by not having a permanent staff in the country, they were dependent on visiting missions and other experts on the ground. It is now clear that until far too late in the day they chose to believe the least alarming reports available and to downplay accounts from private agencies and others which anticipated trouble. They also chose to credit the World Food Programme and the Food and Agricultural Organization of the United Nations with knowing what was happening in Ethiopia.

In the company of other agencies, USAID was positively optimistic about Ethiopia in the early months of 1984. Testifying to a Senate hearing on 1 March, Julia Bloch, head of the Africa Bureau, stated: '... the reports indicate that Ethiopia will be able to meet the food needs of the people within the Government-controlled areas'. This judgement was delivered a month before the Ethiopian Relief and Rehabilitation Commission calculated – quite correctly, as it turned out – that the country would be short of 900,000 tonnes of grain in 1984.

Although senior United States Embassy personnel in Addis Ababa fully shared Washington's distaste for the Ethiopian Government, they seem to have had few doubts about the severity of the approaching famine. A few days after the famous Ghion Hotel donors' meeting with the RRC, the Embassy cabled Washington stating that 'a very serious situation could develop in Ethiopia this year and we will be remiss if we are not adequately informed and prepared ...' The Embassy suggested that USAID conduct an immediate survey into the impact of the famine (the word was used) and the drought. The survey was undertaken and, according to the General Accounting Office, concluded on 11 May, by recommending that the situation should continue to be monitored, but that no additional food should be offered to the Ethiopian Government for the time being. An even worse error of judgement was to follow.

As late as August 1984, USAID was reporting that Ethiopia's food shortages were in check. In response to written questions from a newly formed Select Committee on Hunger, AID officials quoted at length from the report prepared by the joint mission of FAO and WFP experts to Ethiopia in February. We are now familiar with the inadequacies of that report and the misleading rationalizations that were based upon it. Usually proud of its capacity for independent assessment, USAID was on this occasion content to take refuge behind the unmerited optimism of the United Nations.

USAID said that 'although needs in drought-stricken areas might be as great as 450,000 tonnes (through December 1984) only about 125,000 tonnes could be moved given the available transportation resources'. USAID omitted to mention that by Ethiopia's own calculation, needs till the end of 1984 were 900,000 tonnes, and complied with that subordination of people's needs to the availability of trucks to which Dr Kenneth King of the UN had taken such eloquent exception. Worst of all, the figure of 125,000 tonnes now became an immutable target in the eyes of USAID and the United States. 'AID has approved 24,000 tonnes of food for emergency relief in Ethiopia this year and will soon announce further donations,' the agency said. Emergency contributions from other donors were put at over the 90,000 tonnes and fresh donations were likely. 'Thus, current pledges are already within a few thousand tonnes of the level that it is believed possible to deliver, and the balance should be forthcoming in a matter of weeks,' the agency said.

Such blindly reassuring notions seem to have persisted within

USAID until September. Then, as the General Accounting Office reported, three events occurred within two days which at last goaded the agency into a purposeful appreciation of the Ethiopian calamity. On 19 September an unnamed voluntary relief official told the US Embassy in Addis Ababa that he had never seen a situation as bad as that in northern Ethiopia. The same day in Washington, Peter McPherson met private agency officials who told him that they could not handle the quantity of food that was necessary to keep Ethiopia alive and that direct arrangements would have to be made with the Ethiopian Government. On 20 September, a senior Western Ambassador, again unidentified, told the Americans in Addis Ababa that 'Ethiopia is starving to death' and that about 900,000 Ethiopians 'will have died' of malnutrition and related diseases by the end of 1984.

In the middle of all this, Peter McPherson testified on Capitol Hill. He re-emphasized all the problems that the Americans had with Ethiopia, but then added: 'There is no place I feel as frustrated about or as uncomfortable about regarding our response.' With the dam of public concern about to burst in the United States as elsewhere, it was no wonder that McPherson felt uncomfortable.

6

Cathedrals in the Desert

On the day I visited the offices of the European Commission in Addis Ababa, there was no water in the taps. As in many African cities, the population of Addis Ababa has far outgrown its basic services, and a reliable water supply is one of them. The existing system does not bring enough water into the city, and the treatment works in Addis cannot cope with the volume that its 1.5 million people now requires. So the European Community has come to the aid of the city's water-users. At a cost of more than £30 million the Commission is increasing the amount of water that can be piped into Addis Ababa and is then doubling the city's water treatment capacity. The project is the centrepiece of Europe's aid programme to Ethiopia.

When the United States began scaling down its development programme in Ethiopia after the 1974 revolution, it was the European Community that stepped into the breach. Ethiopia has since become the largest recipient of European development assistance, although it also has one of the largest populations among the countries that Europe assists. It is a relationship that is intended to benefit both partners. Some five million jobs in Europe are dependent on exports to the developing world – with developing countries absorbing more than 40 per cent of Europe's exports – and the recession of the early 1980s would have been far worse for Europe without the Third World.

In addition to better water supplies for Addis Ababa, the European Commission is funding two other major projects in Ethiopia. A British construction company, Rush and Tompkins, is the contractor for a huge river diversion scheme which will add to the capacity of a hydro-electric plant west of the capital, and at a cost of more than £14 million the Commission is also financing a power project that will bring high-voltage electricity into the heart of the northern famine zones. Industry in three European countries is benefiting from that scheme. The French are building the transmission lines, the Italians are

68

building the sub-stations and the West Germans are responsible for the transformers.

Projects like these are certainly good for European industry, and they may be good for the creation of a modern state in Ethiopia, but they have precious little to do with what should be Ethiopia's agricultural priorities in the prevention of famine. In a memorable phrase, Edgard Pisani, who until the end of 1984 was European Commissioner for Development, described such projects as 'cathedrals in the desert', and set out during his term of office to redirect European development efforts to where they were most needed. It is now widely recognized that European aid policies have to be changed, and the extent of the famine in countries which the Commission was assisting confirmed the need. In Brussels, André Auclert, director of finance for the Commission's development programme, accepted the inappropriateness of the Addis Ababa water supply scheme. 'It's simply not reasonable to spend such money on one project in the capital,' he said. 'We failed then, and we failed badly.'

If EEC development aid helps European industrialists, EEC food aid is intended first and foremost to benefit European farmers. 'We are not a relief agency,' I was firmly reminded by a Commission official in Addis Ababa. 'We have a food aid programme, which is a very different matter.' The build-up of the European food aid programme was the result not of growing appreciation of the needs of the world's hungry, but of growing food surpluses.

Commission documents have been as straightforward in acknowledging this objective as Commission officials. In 1976, the EEC stated that food aid 'should not be regarded as a simple act of charity'. The costs had to be weighed against 'alternative measures of satisfactorily dealing with unsaleable supplies'. In 1982 the EEC declared in relation to dairy food aid: 'The avowed main objective of this operation is not humanitarian, but financial: the disposal of butter or milk-powder mountains via food aid means savings on storage which offset the cost of the necessary export refunds.' As well as saving on storage costs, food aid is an integral part of commercial sales to deficit countries. It enables and encourages them to buy from Europe's food mountains, and it is written into food aid contracts that commercial purchases should follow. Such an agreement has been part of food aid arrangements between the EEC and Ethiopia for as long as there has been a programme, but the reality of Ethiopia's needs and her lack of

69

foreign exchange have ensured that it has never been enforced.

The distribution of European food aid depends on decisions taken by European Ministers, by the European Parliament, and by the Commission itself in Brussels. Even among Ministers, there is a complex merry-go-round; while Ministers of Finance have to find the money, both Ministers of Agriculture and Ministers of Overseas Development have a say in how the food aid should be used. It is little wonder that the system is slow and inefficient, and little wonder that the most convenient whipping-boys when things go wrong are the Brussels bureaucrats.

At the end of 1984, the European Court of Auditors – a body of which the bureaucrats go in considerable fear – announced their findings on the efficiency of food aid deliveries during 1983. They were not pleased. The year before they had criticized what they called the 'marked increase' of food aid still undelivered at the end of the year. They had been told by the Commission that this situation was going to be rectified. Far from it, the Court of Auditors found. 'The situation at 31 December 1983 had seriously deteriorated as compared with 1982,' their report stated. Less than half the grain allocated in 1983 as food aid was delivered in the course of the year, only a third of the milk powder and about a quarter of the butter oil. The Court of Auditors found that in the case of cereal the time lag between decision and delivery was up to fourteen months, and in the case of butter oil up to nineteen months. 'The Court requests the Commission to review the entire management system for food aid and then to propose both rules and administrative procedures for at least rectifying the defects, which kept recurring and even worsening, at the expense of the poorest countries of all.'

Commission officials replied to this by saying it was not entirely their fault. They had not received authorization to go ahead with the year's food deliveries until 11 July 1983. 'The Commission immediately, that is within three days of adoption of the regulation, took measures for the allocation of almost 70 per cent of the total quantities to countries and organizations,' they said. Things should be better in 1984, the Commission added, because Ministers had adopted the annual implementing regulation 'much earlier' on 7 May, but there could still be improvements. 'In future, the Commission will send its proposals for food aid for the coming year in good time and before the beginning of the year concerned.'

European Commission officials have tried to convince me that

Ethiopia actually benefited from Europe's inefficiencies. Because there were such delays in food shipments in 1983, it meant that food was arriving when it was really needed in 1984. It is not a very persuasive argument, and from the wintry smiles on their faces as they made the point I doubt whether the officials quite believed it themselves. The bulk of food aid authorization to Ethiopia in 1983 was for use on development projects – the EEC became very keen on food-for-work schemes which they judged to be preferable to hand-outs – but what was critically needed in 1984 was food for free distribution through the Relief and Rehabilitation Commission and the foreign relief agencies. Furthermore, the amount of food in the pipeline could have blunted the desire to do more as the crisis built up in 1984. Until the great explosion of public interest in the Ethiopian famine in October, the EEC had committed itself to more food aid for Ethiopia in 1983 than it was intending to give in 1984.

Delays in food deliveries certainly had the effect of making the 1984 figures seem better than they might otherwise have done. As Brussels officials responded in October 1984 to the charge that they had not done enough, press releases were issued stating that from January to September 1984 the Commission had 'delivered or pledged' 116,000 tonnes of cereals. From the bulging grey-green files that fill miles of shelf space in the Commission's headquarters, it is astonishingly difficult to work out what happened when and why. But of those 116,000 tonnes of food, it would seem that at least 62,000 tonnes were from the 1983 programme, delivered late. Until October 1984, there was very little urgency in the EEC's response to the growing crisis.

At the beginning of the year the Commission's office in Addis Ababa had optimistically told Brussels that 'no immediate shortage is expected'. Significant food aid shipments were expected in the first months of the year, the EEC office said, and then fell into the same trap as the United Nations in concluding that Government stocks were available in an emergency: 'AMC [Agricultural Marketing Corporation] ordered to release pre-1983 harvest stocks of 200,000 tonnes', the message from Addis Ababa read. When the Relief and Rehabilitation Commission appealed for massive assistance from the international community in March 1984, there was to be a response of sorts from Brussels, but the reputation of the RRC was not high among European politicians and that imposed additional constraints on EEC generosity.

The Ethiopian revolution has attracted an unholy alliance against it

71

among the politicians of Europe. Conservatives have no time for the régime because it is said to be in the pocket of the Soviet Union, and many on the Left have been inspired by the qualities of the Eritrean and Tigrean guerrilla movements. The 1982 conference of the British Labour Party, for instance, committed a future Labour Government to provide 'direct financial and material support to the Eritrean People's Liberation Front and the Eritrean Relief Association'.

In May 1984, it was the German 'Greens' who sought to discourage the European Commission from showing too much generosity towards Ethiopia. On file at Commission headquarters in Brussels is a letter from Ursula Eid, later a member of the German Parliament, reporting on a trip that she had just made with the Eritrean guerrillas. The letter is headed 'Misuse of food aid by the Ethiopian Government' and concludes with this appeal: 'I urge you to take steps in order to stop the misuse of European Community gifts by the Ethiopian Government.'

On her trip to recently liberated areas of Eritrea in March 1984, said Ms Eid, she had found evidence that 'gifts of the European communities donated to the suffering people of Ethiopia were misused by the Ethiopian army'. In the border town of Tessenei, captured by the guerrillas in January, she had seen 'different items such as oil, butter oil, soap and dishes' in what had been the military stores, and she sent along photographs to Brussels to prove the point. On the coastal strip around Mersa Teklai, which had been an Ethiopian military port until its capture by the guerrillas, Ms Eid had 'found again cartons and tins with butter oil donated by the European Community to the people of Ethiopia'. She added: 'As a citizen of the European communities I feel obliged to report to you these facts and to let you know that unwillingly the European Community is thus indirectly supporting an aggressive army which is leading a war against the Eritrean people.'

Ursula Eid's intervention was probably of less consequence than the campaign that had been building up among Conservative members of the European Parliament. Adam Fergusson, Conservative Member of the European Parliament for Strathclyde West, told Parliament in November 1982: 'Although it is not the Community's habit to tie political strings to humanitarian aid, I wonder whether the Commission would agree that aid to an anti-Western régime which continues to cause so much human misery does not need to be considered.' It was a view to which he stuck. By then no longer a member of the European Parliament, he told an interviewer from the *World in Action* television programme in November 1984 that he was certain that food aid was going to the Ethiopian army. He was still concerned about 'aid to that particular régime which is consorting with our enemies, which has got a pact now with the Libyans and South Yemen, put up to it obviously by the Russians who have bases there. Aid to that sort of régime doesn't aid the West at all.'

A rather more circumspect but still critical view of food aid to Ethiopia was taken by Christopher Jackson, Conservative Member of the European Parliament for Kent East. In late 1982, he told Parliament that the Community should not commit further aid to Ethiopia 'until a full report has been made by the Commission to Parliament'. Again, in April 1983, Mr Jackson wondered 'whether the world's general aid programme to Ethiopia and the Liberation Fronts is not indirectly making possible the continuation of this tragic civil war'.

Political concern over the uses and alleged abuses of food aid to Ethiopia was trumped in March 1983 by a newspaper article that ventilated the wildest possible speculation on the subject. The main front page report in the *Sunday Times* on 27 March was headlined 'Starving Babies' Food Sold for Soviet Arms' and stated that food from the West was not only being diverted to the Ethiopian army, but was also being sent to the Soviet Union 'to help meet the régime's huge arms bills'. In the careful words of a senior colleague on the newspaper, this report by Simon Winchester was 'rather less buttressed by evidence than we might have liked'.

It was apparent from the report that Winchester had not been to Ethiopia to carry out his research, nor had there been much independent research carried out there on his behalf. He relied upon an unnamed 'senior Government official who has recently defected from Ethiopia' and officials of guerrilla movements at war with the régime for his conclusion that food aid was being re-exported to the Soviet Union. Even among critics of the Ethiopian administration, the allegations were regarded as fanciful. Winchester has something of a reputation for colourful reporting, but the damage he did this time was considerable.

The following week, the *Sunday Times* carried a letter from Libby Grimshaw and Hugh Goyder, field directors in Addis Ababa for Save the Children and Oxfam. 'It would be disastrous for the many

73

thousands of people in northern Ethiopia facing famine this year if your report led to any reduction in the amount of food aid being sent by the EEC and other donors,' the two field directors wrote. 'Reports like that in the *Sunday Times* only assist the cynics who firmly believe that all aid to poor countries like Ethiopia goes astray.' Without repeating the allegation that food aid had been re-exported to the Soviet Union – but without withdrawing it, either – Winchester was able in the same issue of the newspaper to quote the Conservative MEP Christopher Jackson as saying that 'reports from a very wide variety of apparently truthful sources all point to the possibility that aid is being diverted'.

The European Commission had already been monitoring the delivery of its food aid to Ethiopia, but newspaper reports and complaints from Parliamentarians stung officials into further action. The EEC office in Addis Ababa was ordered to conduct a fresh investigation and this was carried out by Karl Harbo, a tough-minded Dane who had day-to-day responsibility for the administration of the European food aid programme. 'The delegation is satisfied that all Community Food Aid has been discharged in port and transported inland for distribution,' his report stated. 'Allegations that food aid has been re-exported to third countries are unfounded.' He argued that the unloading of, say, 20,000 tonnes of wheat, including bagging, took between three and four weeks. To re-bag and load it would take the same time. 'This simply cannot take place in such small ports without being noticed by several foreign (Western) employees at the ports, surveyors, and visitors', the report said. Ethiopian ports were not under military control. It was possible, the report added, that people had witnessed the regular onward shipment of food aid from the principal Ethiopian port of Assab to the northern port of Massawa, which serves parts of Government-held Eritrea, but no European aid had ever been transferred in this way. It was also possible, of course, that Winchester's informants were making things up.

On the more plausible allegation that food aid was being diverted within Ethiopia to feed the army, the report stated: 'So far, no conclusive evidence has been produced to show that food aid has been systematically diverted to the armed forces. Aid can be traced from the port of discharge to its final distribution. In the event that improper use of food aid has been made, we believe that it can only have been in very limited quantities, which would not justify any drastic reaction.'

Reports of aid going to the army and militia were to resurface throughout the course of the famine in Ethiopia. It is possible, as the EEC conceded in 1983, that a certain amount had been diverted. The highly respected International Committee of the Red Cross was to allege in 1985 that whole communities in the rebellious northern provinces were being deprived of food and that the militia and army were utilizing food aid. The Relief and Rehabilitation Commission did not help its own cause by being unwilling or unable to account in detail for all the food aid that it was given, and the suspicion lingered that on a matter as vital to the national economy as food aid, a political authority higher than the RRC retained the final say over its distribution. But it is also true that malevolent critics of the Ethiopian régime chose to ignore innocuous explanations whenever food was discovered outside the feeding centres.

On the edges of the great, grim relief camp at Kòrem, a modest market grew up in the course of 1984. 'Market' is perhaps a misnomer for hungry people sitting on the ground in the open with little piles of food, salt and firewood in front of them. After witnessing a distribution of Common Market relief grain in the camp, I saw some of it being sold in this market. A scandal? If they had not been allowed to sell part of their ration, most of them would have been left with a mound of unmilled, uncooked European wheat to live on. If they were to get money to mill it, firewood to cook it on, salt to season it and a few vegetables to eat with it, then they had to be allowed to sell part of their ration. Similarly, much can be made by investigative reporters of the discovery of sacks marked 'Gift of the European Communities to the People of Ethiopia' in places where they should not be. But the bags themselves have a currency in the famine zones and are used and re-used months and years after they have ceased to carry food aid. I have seen grain sacks used as clothes and empty European butter oil tins offered for sale. Hardly a scandal.

What of larger quantities of foreign aid? In the famine areas, food aid has become a wretchedly important part of the local economy and whole communities are dependent on it. When it does not arrive, the RRC has had to 'borrow' grain from other Government departments – like the Ministry of Agriculture and, as we have already seen, the Agricultural Marketing Corporation – against later repayment. This often means that Government departments are in possession of grain firmly stamped 'aid'. Similar 'switch' arrangements have been made, invariably with the agreement of the donors, to save on transport costs.

Then there is the question of food aid in army barracks. The Ethiopian Government has made the same complaint when guerrilla strongholds have been overrun. They too claim to have found quantities of foreign relief aid. It has become an important part of the propaganda war – with the guerrillas being more readily believed than the Government – and it serves once again to obscure the real needs of civilians. The army often has the only properly built store-rooms in the towns; the fact that they hold relief grain does not necessarily mean that soldiers are living off Common Market wheat. Indeed, the Ethiopian army is a privileged body of men and tends to get the more highly prized local cereals like 'teff'.

Corruption of a sort within the RRC has been proved beyond doubt on only one occasion, and it was the *Sunday Times*, though not Simon Winchester, that reported it in December 1983. Again, through a defector, the newspaper acquired a letter written by Shimelis Adugna, then head of the RRC, to a group of his subordinates ordering an elaborate cover-up for the misdirection of a grain consignment from the UN World Food Programme. 'We are aware that having failed in accordance with the agreement the chances of the country getting further food aid could be adversely affected,' Shimelis wrote.

The 16,000 tonnes of food aid should have gone to the country's controversial resettlement programme for refugees from the famine zone. Instead, more than 12,000 tonnes had gone in an exchange arrangement with the Agricultural Marketing Corporation and 3,000 tonnes had gone 'by mistake' to the Ministry of Agriculture. Officials were ordered to present a set of bogus accounts to hoodwink a visiting auditor for the World Food Programme, and then to cover up the cover-up. The last of a complex set of instructions was: 'You are hereby instructed to collect all the documents used by the auditor as soon as he completes his inspection and mark them void.' It was a grotesque fiddle, but it still fell short of proof of diversion to the army, let alone to the Russians. Perhaps that is why this sober report was modestly tucked away on an inside page of the *Sunday Times*. On the evidence of the letter, it is clear that the shipment was indeed used for relief purposes, but not the one specified by the World Food Programme. Instead of resettlement, the RRC had 'used part of the available aid for relief in other provinces that had crop and food shortages. This was not communicated to the donors at the time.'

I suspect that what is different about Ethiopia is not that her institutions are peculiarly corrupt, but that she has a lot of enemies in the West. In a brief tour of the famine areas of Sudan in 1985, I was provided with more eye-witness accounts of the corrupt misuse of food aid than in the course of two much longer tours of Ethiopia. But Sudan's enemies are not to be found in the West. Westerners who are most closely involved with food distribution in Ethiopia give the RRC a fairly clean bill of health, and they seem to do so out of no misplaced wish to please the Ethiopian authorities. 'There is very little natural loss in the aid we give,' said Karl Harbo of the European Commission's office in Addis Ababa. 'One to three per cent loss is really very small. If we insist on the stuff actually being eaten by the recipients, then we might as well give up food aid. In most cases, we're providing the only source of income for these people.' Martin Mock, who was the senior World Food Programme official in Ethiopia in 1983, was quoted as saying that he believed 90 per cent of food aid had gone to the proper recipients. 'I couldn't say that for any of the four other countries I've served in in Africa and the Middle East over the past twenty years,' he said.

In June 1985, Chrisopher Jackson, the European parliamentarian and development spokesman for the Conservative group who had expressed pointed concern about the misuse of European food aid to Ethiopia, arrived in Addis Ababa with a European Parliamentary delegation. At a reception for the visitors, I asked him whether he thought Parliament's criticism had had any effect on the EEC's preparedness to provide food aid for Ethiopia when it was desperately needed in 1984. 'Not the slightest,' he replied, as if I was naive to believe that the European Parliament could have any such influence. But others at the reception disagreed. The British Ambassador to Ethiopia told Mr Jackson that he thought it had had an impact. And Ethiopia's Ambassador to Brussels suggested that Parliamentary opinion may not have cut Europe's aid to Ethiopia, but it ensured that there was nothing extra until much later in the day.

The European Commission has a small budget for emergencies. It was to become much larger when European leaders began to respond to public anxiety over the famine. In the earlier months of 1984, there was a particular problem in its application in Ethiopia. 'We do not consider drought an emergency,' I was told at the Commission's offices in Addis Ababa. 'Only when people start dying of starvation does it become an emergency.'

In the course of 1983, the Commission had made several emergency donations to Ethiopia to combat famine conditions. The Red Cross was given 800 tonnes of food and a consignment of £150,000 worth of French beans. This was topped up with a cash grant of £1.2 million. It did not seem that the response was going to be notably greater in 1984. The food aid allocations were drawn up in accordance with the UN's remarkably long list of twenty-four African countries, and they tended to favour the French-speaking countries of West Africa to which much Common Market food aid had gone from the earliest days of the Community. In March 1984, a cash grant of £1.5 million was made to Ethiopia through UNDRO, the Office of the United Nations Disaster Relief Co-ordinator. And that, more or less, was going to be that for 1984.

As part of his forlorn tour of the major donors, Dawit Wolde Giorgis of the Relief and Rehabilitation Commission arrived in Brussels in May. The RRC had made its appeal for 450,000 tonnes of food aid two months earlier, and he was already alarmed at the world's lack of response. Dawit had some hopes of getting assistance from the European Commission, which was a major donor to Ethiopia. A request had accordingly been submitted for 115,000 tonnes of grain, 15,000 tonnes of milk powder and 2,500 tonnes of butter oil. There may have been little realistic expectation of getting such huge amounts, but it was an eloquent means of expressing the magnitude of the country's needs. The response from the Commission was poor.

Food aid officials had made their allocations before Dawit arrived, and Ethiopia was already down on the list for 18,000 tonnes of grain. In deference to those who argued that hand-outs created an undesirable dependency on foreign food, the Commission had further stipulated that the 18,000 tonnes should be earmarked for a food-for-work development scheme. But what Dawit needed was food for emergency relief, and he needed it quickly. So the Commission made an exception and agreed that Ethiopia could utilize the 18,000 tonnes of grain for famine relief. This technical change in a donation that had already been agreed was hardly a munificent response to a request for 115,000 tonnes, but it was better than nothing. Ethiopia was also to receive 1,400 tonnes of milk powder – less than one tenth of what it had asked for – and 500 tonnes of butter oil – just a fifth of what had been requested.

The 18,000 tonnes of emergency aid can now be traced to their destination. The grant was approved by the Council of Ministers on 17 June, but because of the Community's elaborate tendering procedures, even for emergency assistance, it was not identified, loaded and shipped for another six weeks. On 27 July 1984, the shipment left Le Havre on a Greek freighter which then called at ports in the eastern Mediterranean to take on jute and textiles for the Ethiopian Textile Corporation. It arrived at the Ethiopian port of Assab in early September. So poor had been the response from other donors to the RRC's March appeal that the shipment represented virtually the only grain available for distribution in the famine areas. For thousands, it was a lifeline. What food aid there was in Korem in October 1984 was from the European Commission.

When public opinion finally demanded action on the famine, the European Commission doubled and redoubled its efforts on behalf of Ethiopia. A further 25,000-tonne food-for-work shipment was authorized and converted into emergency use for famine relief, and in November alone emergency cash grants were made which were six times what had been approved in the previous ten months. Brussels officials worked throughout the Christmas holiday to give expression to the 'Dublin Plan' agreed by European leaders in early December. Unspent budgets in the industrial and social sectors were suddenly discovered, stripped, and utilized for famine relief, and the small staff in the Commission's Addis Ababa office was run off its feet.

'It was fantastic,' Karl Harbo recalled. 'You had this feeling of immense public support in Europe. And the spirit here was incredible. Everyone was positive about doing things. Before, you could never really talk about the problem itself; it was always a question of how to present the problem. There was simply nothing that could not be done at that time. Now of course, we're back in the old routine.'

At the end of 1984, Edgard Pisani, the former French Agriculture Minister who had been Europe's Development Commissioner since 1981, was replaced in the regular switch-over of national commissioners. His next job – requiring no less diplomacy – was French Government Representative in the troubled territory of New Caledonia. It was Pisani who, as Development Commissioner, had argued the need for European development aid to be devoted to grass-roots agriculture in preference to 'cathedrals in the desert', and that outlook was reflected in new treaty arrangements signed between the Commission and the Governments of developing countries in

December 1984. Pisani had insisted on more of a 'policy dialogue' with Third World Governments that would respect their sovereign rights, but in which the Commission would exercise its 'right and duty' to vet the effectiveness of future development projects. In plain language there would be no more money for grandiose urban water supply or electrification programmes when people were starving.

Pisani had some equally trenchant things to say about the workings of European institutions when faced with a crisis. Responding to one of his last debates in the European Parliament in November 1984, he contrasted the capacity of national Governments to react to disaster with that of the Commission: 'We are caught up in a much more complex network of institutions, and this complexity and this rigidity make it difficult for us to tackle emergency aid issues,' he said. 'How is it possible to blame an institution for not using funds which it has not been given? We were not given the funds! ... Let us try to see, on the contrary, how the Community makes everything impossible – because it has become self-paralysing, a victim of self-induced paralysis, because it is incapable of advancing, due to member states' mutual distrust and, by increasing the number of procedures, makes everything impossible.'

Among the measures that Pisani proposed to ensure a more effective response to future emergencies was what he called 'a new definition of the relationship between food aid and the Common Agriculture Policy'. It was a crucial point that had exercised public concern during the autumn: the build-up of massive grain surpluses in Europe at a time of starvation in Africa. What was it that prevented the grain surpluses of Europe being applied to the famine areas of Africa?

7

Moving Mountains

At the beginning of August 1984, Marcus Thompson, one of Oxfam's disasters officers, left Britain for Ethiopia. Although the country was regarded by the voluntary agencies as being in a state of virtually permanent crisis, his was not exactly a disasters assignment. First, he was taking over for a period from the field director, Hugh Goyder, who was due in Britain on leave. Secondly, Oxfam had a good deal of money that really ought to be spent in Ethiopia. The Independent Television documentary 'Seeds of Despair' and some BBC news footage had been the springboard for a successful Disasters Emergency Committee appeal in July, and Oxfam had already netted around £2 million as its share of the proceeds.

There was to be complaint later from the Ethiopians that it had been images of their starving that had mobilized public generosity in the West, and yet it was not always Ethiopians who benefited. Funds had been utilized elsewhere in Africa, and sometimes not even there. Commissioner Dawit of the RRC told a donors' meeting in October that funds raised 'for the sake of our suffering multitudes have been withheld or diverted elsewhere', and the issue was one of the few on which Colonel Mengistu himself cared publicly to pronounce during the course of the emergency. He told an interviewer from Canadian Broadcasting that the people who were raising the money 'should establish direct contact with ourselves. If they don't, then there is the likelihood that this money has been used for other purposes.'

Oxfam's programme in Ethiopia was aimed at development, not relief. The agency had started famine relief work in Wollayta, south of Addis Ababa, where it already had a number of development projects, but the crisis there was easing and there was little chance of being able effectively to spend even a chunk of the £2 million. It was part of Thompson's brief to see if there was anything else that Oxfam could usefully do. It did not take him too long to come up with an answer.

In a telex to his Oxford headquarters on 8 August, Thompson stated: 'Everyone we speak to from the RRC to the voluntary agencies is very alarmed at the lack of grain in the country for general ration distribution.' Others in the field concurred. Mark Bowden, Save the Children's Deputy Overseas Director, who was also visiting Ethiopia, was saying similar things to his own head office. 'There is now little chance of avoiding a famine of at least the scale of 1973-4,' he wrote. 'What is more depressing is that the actual state of preparedness among the agencies here is minimal, with what appears to be almost total lack of co-ordination from the centre.' He too concluded that the fundamental need was emergency grain: 'It is obvious from the food aid figures that relief imports will not be sufficient for any large-scale relief distribution.'

Thompson's decisive contribution was to propose that Oxfam step into the grain business itself and in some measure usurp the functions of mightier United Nations and Government agencies by buying its own shipload of food. If the big agencies were incapable of feeding Ethiopia, then Oxfam would show the way. 'If substantial funds are available,' his telex to Oxford continued, 'I suggest we consider purchase and delivery to Assab of substantial shipment of grain, say, 10,000-20,000 tonnes.' The proposal and the fact that it was subsequently adopted and executed by Oxfam was an early pointer to a general lesson of the Ethiopian famine: that the voluntary agencies had now emerged as the most vital, if less well-endowed, component of the whole aid network; and that for all their money, carpeted offices and well-paid officials, the big aid agencies of the United Nations and Western Governments had failed in what the public had taken to be their most important duty – to stop people starving.

Considering that the purchase and shipment of 10,000 tonnes of grain would cost more than the £2 million that Oxfam was expecting from the July appeal, Thompson's was a staggering proposal. In fact, at the end of his telex he thought it wise to add the postscript 'Above suggestion is no joke.' He justified it on the following grounds. It would 'address the most urgent and directly felt need (albeit only a small contribution overall)'; it 'might galvanize WFP [the World Food Programme of the United Nations] into more useful deliveries'; and it would enable voluntary agencies to continue with relief programmes that depended on fast-dwindling supplies of relief grain. Since Oxfam, in the company of other charities, lives by public subscription,

Thompson added a further justification. 'Incidentally, this would be a mighty PR coup both in Britain and in Ethiopia,' he wrote.

Oxfam's disasters office is run by old India hands. Marcus Thompson had been the agency's field director in Nagpur; Tony Vaux, who was responsible for the excellent evaluation of who-did-what in the famine, had been field director in Ahmadabad; and Dick Copeland, disasters co-ordinator, had been Oxfam's man in the capital, Delhi. It now fell to Copeland to deal with Thompson's extraordinary notion that the charity, whose offices are still above a laundry in the Banbury Road, should actually be in the business of wholesale grain export. Two things occurred to him straight away. First, that this was not Oxfam's job. Second, that a bumper grain harvest was being brought in around him in Oxfordshire, and that it should not prove too difficult to devote a tiny part of it to the victims of famine in Ethiopia. He reckoned without the rules and regulations of the intervening bureaucracies.

Copeland's first telephone calls were to the Overseas Development Administration in London. This is the Government department, part of the Foreign and Commonwealth Office, which disburses British aid. Since Britain is not traditionally a food exporter – this has changed in recent years under the influence of Common Market subsidies – and since British officials have accepted arguments that food aid can do as much harm as good, the British Government sees itself as a rather reluctant provider of food aid. But ODA is still responsible for about 110,000 tonnes of food aid a year, and Copeland thought there might be some of that available. He was disappointed. 'They said they were very sorry,' Copeland recalled, 'but they only had 5,000 tonnes left and they couldn't give us any.'

Next, Dick Copeland tried the European Commission in Brussels which presided over the Continent's grain mountain. Here too the year's allocations had been virtually used up, and it was far too early for next year's. Of the one million tonnes that the EEC disburses each year in food aid – much of it, as we have seen, for budgetary relief rather than the relief of hunger – they only had what was described as a 'negligible quantity' left, around one or two per cent of the total. Copeland wanted exactly that quantity, between 10,000 and 20,000 tonnes, to be given either to Oxfam or direct to the Ethiopian Government. 'I was told it was not possible,' he said to me later. 'They said they had no reserves. There were some cereals for development

83

work and that was it.' It was surprising what impact a few weeks of sustained publicity was to have on the same European institutions. When European leaders met in Dublin later in the year, they sanctioned the delivery of 1,200,000 tonnes of relief grain to Africa. Some of it was entirely new aid and not the re-working of existing budgets. But in August, Dick Copeland was out of luck with his 10,000 tonnes.

Through Oxfam offices around the world, Copeland also made contact with other major aid-givers and impressed upon them the desperate urgency of food supplies in Ethiopia. The Australian Government pleaded that it was sending food supplies to countries in the Sahel, and the Canadians said they had already despatched 20,000 tonnes via the UN World Food Programme. Predictably Oxfam received the shortest shrift from the United States Administration. It was told bluntly that there was 'no possibility' of grain being available for Ethiopia.

Marcus Thompson's original plan that Oxfam might defray the expense of the grain shipment by involving other voluntary agencies fell upon more fertile ground. Norwegian Church Aid and Redd Barna, the Norwegian Save the Children, came up with major contributions, and Oxfam itself was let off relatively lightly with £500,000. It was still the agency's largest-ever grant in forty years of development and relief work. In political impact alone, it was worth the price.

Even Oxfam exhibits on occasions the characteristics of a cautious bureaucracy, and there was debate within the organization as to whether to publicize the grant and the reasons for it. Some argued that this would upset the agency's relations with the Government, as if that were a laudable ground for inaction. Like other private agencies, Oxfam has profited from the dismal failures of official aid, and the British Government is using it more and more as a channel for its own funds. But there are dangers in this process, accentuated perhaps by the recent appointment of notably Establishment figures to the most senior posts in the agency. On this occasion dangerous chumminess with Government was averted, the Oxfam shipment was publicized, and the Overseas Development Administration was duly upset.

The Oxfam press release of 10 September described the grant as 'a bid to galvanize Western Governments into sending urgent grain supplies to Ethiopia'. The agency's Overseas Director, Michael

Harris, was quoted as saying: 'Oxfam has been obliged to make this gesture to the Ethiopian people because of the failure of grain-surplus countries in the West to send adequate emergency food aid to Ethiopia. In most drought disasters we can normally count on large-scale quantities of staple food being provided by donor governments or the EEC either directly or through the UN's World Food Programme.' This, he said, had allowed voluntary agencies like Oxfam to concentrate on special feeding programmes for particularly vulnerable groups and to plug gaps in health care and water supply. Oxfam had tried to get access to the bumper grain stocks piling up in Britain and in Europe, but had failed. 'Despite every effort by Oxfam it appears impossible to secure free supplies through the normal channels for emergency food aid supplies for Third World countries,' he concluded.

Oxfam's initiative focused attention on the 1984 grain harvest in Europe, which by September was already a record-breaker. Even Britain, which a decade before had been a grain importer, was set to beat its previous best harvest by almost four million tonnes. It was an issue that was to put British official spokesmen on the defensive, a posture that they maintained for most of the Ethiopian emergency.

'When in doubt pooh-pooh the idea' is a reliable bureaucratic maxim. My earliest record of the Government's response to the idea that part of British and European grain surpluses might go to save people's lives in Africa is a statement issued by the Eastern and Western Africa Department of the Overseas Development Administration on 21 August 1984. It was to be repeated a number of times over the next two months, sometimes as a press release from the ODA, sometimes as part of a Ministerial speech. The original version is worth quoting in full.

'It has been suggested', the statement began in that tone of pained superiority adopted by the British civil service when in a corner, 'that the answer to the famine in Ethiopia and elsewhere is to transfer wholesale as aid the various agricultural surpluses generated in the Community. This would have serious drawbacks. Food of this kind from Europe has to be bought with aid funds and is very expensive to ship, slow to distribute and often unfamiliar to the local diet. It can generate "aid dependence" and undermines demands to revive and develop local farming which alone can prevent famine in future. We must be selective about what we provide; even so it may often be better, cheaper and quicker to buy it in other African countries than in Britain.'

It was a shocking piece of obfuscation. First, of course, no one had ever proposed shipping everything that was in surplus in Europe to Africa. What was being requested was additional shipments of grain and of supplementary foods like milk powder and butter oil which were already European aid staples. Second, the storage of European grain surpluses had become so expensive that there was a respectable case for arguing that they should be given away. Third, the unfamiliarity of European wheat to the Ethiopian diet proved to be of small consequence when the alternative was death by starvation. Fourth, it is a harsh rejoinder to a starving man to tell him that in the opinion of the ODA feeding him will generate 'aid dependence'. Fifth, neither the British Government nor the EEC sought to buy grain in quantity locally in Africa. Finally, by the time European leaders met in Dublin at the end of the year to consider the political implications of failing to do more, it was decided that European surpluses should be pressed a little more whole-heartedly into the relief of hunger.

Timothy Raison, Minister for Overseas Development, utilized this civil service brief when he spoke in early October, but by then the tone had changed as ODA began to acknowledge the peculiar severity of the Ethiopian famine. 'People ask me why we cannot simply ship our European food surpluses,' he told a group of his constituents at an improbable weekend meeting at the Princes Risborough Chamber of Trade. 'That is in effect what we do when we give cereals food aid.' He stuck to all the arguments for doing nothing, and then added: 'But in the short term there is no alternative to food aid and we shall continue to act.'

The Oxfam shipment now finally caught up with ODA. Having turned down the idea of helping out in August, they reconsidered the matter six weeks later. That became the pattern of the British Government's response to famine: to follow the lead of others rather than take the initiative. Diplomacy played a part on this occasion. Hugh Goyder, Oxfam's Addis Ababa field director, enjoyed good relations with Brian Barder, British Ambassador to Ethiopia, and Barder was anxious that Britain do its best. He argued for a response to the Oxfam initiative and got one. ODA agreed to put 3,000 tonnes of grain aboard the SS *Elpis* which sailed from Hull on 10 October. It was a sure sign of the moral lead which the charities had established over the official agencies that the British Government should ask for space in the hold of an Oxfam ship.

As the famine crisis became the focus of public concern, the ODA made more and more of a virtue of its association with the voluntary agencies. Many of the funds from the ODA's own Disasters Unit were funnelled through the charities, and the Minister kept emphasizing that he had doubled the sums committed to development work through them. Too great a emphasis on this would have been out of place. At £5 million a year, it amounted to only half a per cent of Britain's declining aid budget.

Government help for voluntary agencies promoted a process of merit by association in which many big official agencies joined. The World Bank, biggest of them all, set up a special unit to liaise with the voluntary agencies and senior officials from its Paris office were seen dining Oxfam and others in some of London's better restaurants in 1985. It alarmed the old guard. 'There's a big question mark over the future of the voluntary agencies now,' Michael Harris, Oxfam's retiring Overseas Director, told me. 'There's a real danger that they too – like the UN – will become too bureaucratic.' The dangers were expressed best of all by the development economist Susan George at a conference of the voluntary agencies in Dakar, Senegal, in May 1985. 'Beware the agency that has so much money that you – and the people you want to help – could easily drown in it,' she said. She accused Governments of wanting 'to spend infinitely less on overseas aid than they did before, but to get enormous public credit by giving whatever tiny sums remain to the non-governmental organizations ... I implore you to guard your independence,' she concluded. 'Just remember, if somebody still dislikes you, you must be doing something right.'

By September 1984, the independent agencies on the ground in Addis Ababa were becoming increasingly shrill in their representations to the big donors. Early in the month, a team linked to the International Disasters Institute telexed the World Food Programme in Rome, pointing out that Ethiopia's Relief Commission had just released its final reserve stock of 7,100 tonnes. It estimated that 3.5 million drought victims would need 58,000 tonnes a month to avert mass starvation. Even though the figure for famine victims was to rise substantially, the IDI's estimate of need was widely adopted. 'We conclude that in the absence of sufficient international aid there are likely to be three peaks of starvation deaths,' the telex ran. 'Firstly July to September. Secondly December to March 1985 (assuming some extra shipments by March). Thirdly from the middle of 1985 up to the harvest period August–November 1985.' As things turned out, the death rate remained very high well beyond September 1984, but the worst of the IDI's subsequent fears were unrealized. By then, international assistance had stabilized and reduced the death rate.

The failure to avert the 1984 Ethiopian tragedy was felt keenly by some of the private agencies, and their evaluation can be more readily trusted than that of the bigger bureaucracies. Oxfam, for one, reproached itself. It admitted in evidence to the House of Commons Foreign Affairs Committee that the crisis had come 'quicker than we thought it would. We were caught napping.' Hugh Goyder, Oxfam's field director throughout this period in Addis Ababa, was prepared to take his share of the blame. The problem, he told me, lay in the fact that he continued to concentrate too much on Oxfam's own programme in Ethiopia and to subscribe to Oxfam's development priorities when there was a full-scale disaster mounting in the country. 'I blame myself for having taken too much of a worm's eye view until September,' he said. He had relied too heavily on the expertise and judgement of others. 'Only from September did we realize how badly the UN had let us down,' he added.

The agency best placed to monitor the mounting tragedy was Save the Children Fund, with its relief camp in Korem. At a meeting on 3 September of the Christian Relief Development Association, umbrella organization for private agencies, the SCF field director David Alexander reported that the number of children receiving daily feeding in Korem had begun to increase rapidly in the second week of August. In Rome, I was told by an FAO official that agencies like SCF had not done enough to publicize their findings in the field. 'Crucial information on nutrition status was not collected,' the official said. 'It certainly wasn't reported here at the FAO.' This criticism speaks more eloquently of failures within the UN system than among the relief agencies. There was a representative of the World Food Programme in attendance at most CRDA meetings during 1984, including the one in early September at which Alexander spoke.

Having criticized its own role, Oxfam also queried that of others. In his evaluation of the early months of the famine, Tony Vaux wondered whether the absence from Ethiopia of key SCF personnel during periods of 1984 had meant a lack of emphasis on the increasing evidence of famine in Wollo. 'Clearly, SCF were scarcely more alert to the seriousness of the situation than Oxfam, in spite of a close involvement in Wollo,' the Vaux report said.

There was also criticism of the Christian Relief Development Association, which as the co-ordinator of charitable relief efforts in Ethiopia might have been expected to play a decisive part in the early mobilization of opinion abroad, as well as of relief work on the ground. The International Disaster Institute commented unfavourably on the CRDA. With the famine approaching, said the IDI, 'the prospect should have been appalling enough for even a moderate probability of such an event to have triggered detailed contingency planning. It did not, seemingly because people running relief operations in the midst of emergencies get caught up in day-to-day management problems and do not seem to have the time or the inclination to think very far ahead in terms of probabilities.' The Vaux report from Oxfam made a similar point. 'The CRDA acted as pool of information,' it said, 'but failed to plot the overall course and the seriousness of the food deficits.'

If there were any gaps in SCF's earlier performance, they were firmly plugged in September. When the CRDA met again at the end of the month, to assess a still deteriorating situation, it was Dr John Seaman, Save the Children's chief medical officer with immense experience of Ethiopia, who made the running in the formulation of a vital Association initiative. This was an emphatic telex signed by eighteen of the CRDA member organizations which was subsequently adopted and distributed by UNDRO, the Office of the United Nations Disaster Relief Co-ordinator in Geneva. The telex expressed the 'deep concern' of the eighteen private agencies at the gravity of the famine in Ethiopia and at the 'desperate shortage of relief food' in the country. It requested 'immediate and extraordinary action by all relief donors to meet the crisis'.

For the first time some target figures were adopted for relief assistance needed to feed all or most of the hungry. The UN's evasive arithmetic, by which people's needs were assessed on the basis of how much the donor community might provide, was at last abandoned. The CRDA telex quoted World Food Programme estimates that 100,000 tonnes of relief supplies were due to reach Ethiopia by the end of 1984. 'This is sufficient to feed the affected population for only 30 days,' the telex said. 'Not less than 60,000 tonnes of relief food will be required per month until December 1985. There is no doubt that if substantial quantities of food are not forthcoming immediately, hundreds of thousands of people will die. This can be avoided.'

The telex concluded by declaring that 'only immediate and massive action can arrest this famine'. The agencies, of course, had no means of wishing tens of thousands of tonnes of grain to the famine areas that quickly, and hundreds of thousands probably did die as a result. It was still a month or so before BBC News items forced the big donors into appropriate action. But through their action the CRDA had at last quantified the needs. The excuses offered by donors for doing so little were beginning to wear thin.

8

'The Oxygen of Publicity'

'Dawn, and as the sun breaks through the piercing chill of night on the plain outside Korem, it lights up a biblical famine, now, in the twentieth century. This place, say workers here, is the closest thing to hell on earth.' The first of Michael Buerk's reports from northern Ethiopia ran on the BBC Six O'Clock News on 23 October 1984. The BBC said that its footage was subsequently shown by 425 of the world's broadcasting organizations with a potential audience of 470 million people. An evocative commentary combined with the stunning camerawork of Mohammed Amin brought world-wide public attention to bear on mass starvation that should have been prevented. It was then that public opinion forced the hand of the aid bureaucracies and their political masters into making a response to match the calamity. For that service alone, Buerk and Amin richly deserved the professional awards that they received.

Michael Buerk had his introduction to the Ethiopian famine a few months earlier. In July, ITV showed 'Seeds of Despair', an hour-long documentary which had been several months in the making and which was to be the basis of a famine appeal in Britain. The BBC was approached by the Disasters Emergency Committee of the big British charities to screen its own appeal at the same time. The old rivalry between news organizations reasserted itself, and BBC News set out to pip ITV in the famine stakes.

Six days before the ITV documentary was shown, Michael Buerk sent an urgent telex from Johannesburg to his friend Paddy Coulter, Oxfam's head of communications. 'Help,' it began. 'Have had request from Beeb in London relating to an appeal, to be televised next Thursday, entitled "Famine in Africa". You will presumably know more about this than me (you could scarcely know less). The Beeb had the nice idea of satelliting in a piece to camera of me with drought victims doing a "And today here in ..." to be incorporated in the appeal. Presumably at a cost that would keep

Upper Volta in asparagus for years. TV News thought I could also knock off a drought package for that night's Nine O'Clock News.' What Buerk needed was 'urgent advice on where I can leap in and out of quickly with pictures of harrowing drought victims etc. to be edited and satellited from either Jo'burg or Nairobi. Apparently money no object, nor distance, only time.'

Visas for travel to Third World countries, particularly Marxist ones, can take weeks to materialize. But Ethiopia was still the best bet, and Oxfam enjoyed good relations with the Ethiopian authorities. With a British appeal in prospect, they were quick to oblige. Buerk and his crew fetched up at Addis Ababa airport and within fifteen minutes were on the road to Wollayta, a day's drive south of the capital where Buerk's 'pictures of harrowing drought victims' could most easily be found. What Buerk later described as a 'series of miracles' enabled him to film in southern Ethiopia, return to Addis Ababa, fly to Nairobi and satellite his reports so that they were in time both to help the launch of the British famine appeal and to pre-empt the ITV documentary by a few hours.

Rivalry between Britain's two main television channels played a big part in public awareness of food emergencies in Africa. For a period in 1980 for instance, two journalists based in East Africa, Brian Barron of the BBC and David Smith of ITN, regularly outdid each other in the discovery of fresh horrors in northern Uganda. In spring 1983, rival teams were taken on virtually the same tour of northern Ethiopia. An appeal was launched on that occasion which netted just under £2 million. Despite television's remorseless eye for the worst cases of malnutrition – and harrowing pictures can always be found – the public demonstrated discerning judgement on the relative gravity of famine. In the three months that followed the famine appeal of July 1984 the British gave almost £10 million, and just when the Disasters Emergency Committee wanted to close the appeal in October the public insisted on giving all over again. In the next four months British relief agencies raised another £50 million.

Television's appetite for the extreme had not helped in the more complex business of alerting people to the build-up of famine. Save the Children Fund press officers quoted an ITV reporter in 1984 as apologizing for having concentrated on political rather than humanitarian questions during a visit to Ethiopia early in the year.

'There were no acute cases of starvation to film,' he said, 'so it wasn't news.'

The written media were no better. A few senior journalists from the United States went to find out what was happening in Ethiopia. Their British counterparts were largely uninterested in the matter until their readers began responding to television pictures. A letter from Save the Children Fund to the Ethiopian Ambassador in London in May 1984 recorded the press office's frustration. 'As I think you are aware, we made every possible effort to obtain media interviews on the situation in Korem featuring the field director, Libby Grimshaw, on her return to this country,' the letter said. 'Sadly none of the journalists we approached showed much interest, although BBC TV Nine O'Clock News on 16 May quoted her statement that the humanitarian situation had worsened a good deal.'

When Ethiopia's famine hit the headlines, it did so because of the relationship between private relief agencies and the television companies. Michael Buerk's visit in July was accomplished through Oxfam. In news coverage in October and beyond, the relief agencies provided most of the reference points – up-to-date information, places to visit, interviewees in the field and at home, and a means of response for concerned viewers. Our own *TV Eye* film 'Bitter Harvest', made for Thames Television and transmitted on 25 October, had it origins in Oxfam's decision to purchase large quantities of grain for Ethiopia. Oxfam helped us secure visas, and although we were happy to pay all the bills, we depended on Oxfam and Save the Children in Ethiopia for transport in the famine area.

'Bitter Harvest' was caught up in that autumn ritual, an ITV technicians' dispute. Oxfam and Save the Children appealed to union and management 'to show humanitarian support by allowing this powerful film to be shown on national television as a special case'. Thames prepared to transmit the film on its own management-run local service, but the union was adamant that it would be given no special dispensation. Alan Sapper, general secretary of the Association of Cinematograph, Television and Allied Technicians, declined even to receive telephone calls on the subject from Guy Stringer, Oxfam's director, and Hugh McKay, Overseas Director of Save the Children. Then the *London Standard* newspaper ran a front-page story detailing the ACTT's action, provoking what the paper described as 'an amazing U-turn'. Striking film editors finished work on the film as unpaid volunteers and it was given a national showing. 'We fully share the concern of the two charities that the widest possible support should be obtained for the relief of this terrible famine,' Alan Sapper said. It was another example of the impact of publicity on bureaucracy.

Some experts were concerned about the journalist's role in the reporting of famine. The environmental agency Earthscan was rather pompous on the subject. 'The general public's impression of disasters is formed not by relief agencies, but by journalists, who are rarely experts in this area, but who are often called upon to interpret quickly both the event and the relief efforts for the rest of the world,' said Earthscan. 'Is it enough to merely count the dead and describe the damage? Or is it a journalist's job to look behind the scenes of destruction to expose ways in which people, politics and social systems have been responsible for any given disaster?'

Among agencies working in the field there is a different concern: that they may be too dependent on the media. In his study of the build-up to the famine from which I have already quoted, Tony Vaux of Oxfam found that the ITV documentary 'Seeds of Despair', rather than the emergency on the ground, may have prompted the major charity appeal in July. 'Is waiting for the media inevitable,' he wondered, 'or can we be ready to respond without them?' He pointed out that news film had launched the spring 1983 appeal, and of 'Seeds of Despair' he concluded: 'Once again it was the media, not the monitoring, that brought awareness.' Sometimes, Vaux argued, it is the arrival of the television cameras that persuade even experienced relief workers that there is an emergency, a view confirmed in a letter received by Oxfam from a missionary worker in the southern Ethiopian famine zone. 'Our view from the beginning of this emergency has been that supplementary feeding centres are only a stop-gap solution, and the real problem was out in the countryside. This point was brought home to us by the BBC and Marcus Thompson [Oxfam disasters officer].'

Michael Buerk's powerful reporting in October 1984 set off a chain reaction of concern in which the whole world joined. Individual acts of charity were the most striking. A couple in Scotland auctioned the contents of their home for the Ethiopian famine appeal after seeing the television pictures. They kept a table, some chairs and a bed for

94

themselves, until the person who had bought their dresser charitably returned it to them. As an example of American compassion, Vice-President Bush pointed to a little girl called Sandra Nathan from Brooksville, Florida, who had given her life savings to the charity CARE. Sandra was six and her savings were $5. A group of Vietnamese boat people in a Hong Kong transit camp collected 6,125 Hong Kong dollars – about £600 – for the local Ethiopian famine relief fund.

The rest of the world's media scrambled to respond. When I returned to Ethiopia in 1985, I saw a small white truck in Addis Ababa with these words written in huge lettering along the side: '24 HOUR TELEVISION. LOVE SAVES THE EARTH'. It belonged, I discovered, to Nippon Television, which had devoted part of the proceeds from a recent Telethon to the famine. Not only that; in a comprehensive Japanese gesture, Nippon Television had decided to open and run its own feeding centre. With the help of more established relief agencies, they had reached a formal agreement with the Ethiopian Relief Commission to operate in the town of Waldia. In June 1985, they were feeding 1,200 adults and children, with 150 under intensive care. They had brought a Japanese doctor and five nurses to run the camp. Its administrator, Noriyuki Kunioka, was also a producer of the original television programme. 'I find it very interesting,' he told me. 'Setting up a camp, visualizing what it will be like, is similar to putting a television programme together.'

Not all of television's involvement in the famine was as positive. In November 1984, a French television station ran a 'Trucks for Hope' convoy through the Sahara to take medicines and other supplies to countries in the Sahel. It was described as the 'humanitarian equivalent of the Paris–Dakar rally', and involved spending almost as much money keeping the convoy in satellite contact with France as bringing relief to the needy. 'We chose the marathon format in order to keep the public in suspense,' explained the organizer. Some of the medical equipment carried on the convoy was said to have been shaken to bits by the need to maintain a good speed over appalling roads, and local officials complained that what they called a 'road-race' was diverting attention from serious relief work.

The producers of the NBC hospital soap opera 'St Elsewhere' conceived the bright idea of shooting a segment of one of their shows in an Ethiopian relief camp. Arrangements were made by the Red

Cross to take two writers and an executive producer on a four-day tour of the camps. Having spent one night in a rural hotel in Ethiopia, the team told their Red Cross escort that they would prefer to skip the rest and return to Addis Ababa. They left the country the next day, never to return. The reality of famine was even less comfortable than its televised presentation.

Mohammed Amin, the brilliant cameraman responsible for the BBC's initial coverage in October, returned to make a film called 'African Calvary' which was shown in Britain during Easter 1985. It was a sort of hymn to starvation which from several senior relief officials earned the less flattering title 'African Cavalry' for the relentlessness of its imagery. It was also remarkable for the numbing platitudes of world leaders on the subject of starvation. Mrs Thatcher's contribution, delivered in a tone of emphatic sympathy, was that 'we have to try to teach the basics of long-term husbandry'. It was an ironic observation. Ethiopians had already survived many years of crop failure through careful husbandry, and Mrs Thatcher's Government had set its face against long-term development help for Ethiopia.

No world disaster would have been complete without a popular newspaper battle. Rupert Murdoch's *Sun* started a '*Sun* to the Rescue' campaign and collected £100,000 for the child victims of the famine. 'We know that *Sun* readers love children – whatever their colour or creed,' declared the *Sun*, as if they were not entirely sure. Robert Maxwell, new proprietor of the *Daily Mirror*, went one better by campaigning for funds and starting his own airlift. A week before the BBC television pictures were screened, there was only modest interest at the *Mirror* when we told them that 100 people were dying daily of starvation in Korem, but now Maxwell was taking a proprietorial interest in the matter. He was to launch similar funds for the Bradford and Brussels football disasters in 1985.

Maxwell got the *Daily Mirror*'s first 'Mercy Flight' off the ground on 31 October. His friendship with Lord King, chairman of British Airways, ensured a competitive charter price of £32,000 for the TriStar's trip to Addis Ababa and back. Maxwell himself was on the flight in his role as world diplomat. But another of his many roles as chairman of Oxford United Football Club found him still in the team dressing-room at half-time when he was due at Heathrow to board the *Mirror*'s 'Mercy Flight' to Ethiopia. He was summoned from the match by a telephone call from the airport and an irritated

Lord King shepherded him aboard the plane. Maxwell boasted later that he had the second half of the match relayed to his hotel room in Addis Ababa, but the process by which this technical feat was achieved remained unclear.

In its campaign against Maxwell, the magazine *Private Eye* alleged in July 1985 that only £500,000 of the £2 million collected by the *Daily Mirror* had been spent and that the rest was gaining interest in an account at the Royal Bank of Scotland. As is so often the case with *Private Eye*, the facts were otherwise. The appeal fund never reached £2 million, and it was perhaps inexcusable journalistic licence on the *Mirror*'s part to suggest that it had ever got above £1.7 million. By the summer of 1985, around £1.5 million – not all of it spent – had been committed to a worthy water-drilling scheme in the famine zone. The money left over – on deposit at Coutts Bank, not the Royal Bank of Scotland – would be needed to maintain the drilling programme in Ethiopia.

Popular journalism of the type that may encourage public generosity is a mixed blessing in the field. A volunteer worker in Sudan was quoted by the *Guardian* in March 1985 as complaining: 'The freelance photographers are the worst. We had one bastard here, a Japanese, who spent three hours crouched by an old woman, so he could get a picture of her death.' Andrew Timpson, the Save the Children Fund field director in Sudan, saw another problem: 'It's not just the money they bring in. Television is also providing a forceful education for the public. But I'm concerned that television may not be moving on from showing starving children to reporting on the rehabilitation and development work in agriculture that can prevent starvation.'

There was a mawkishness to much popular newspaper coverage that relief workers found objectionable. In the publicity that surrounded '*Mirror* Mercy Flight No. 2', the newspaper featured a British Red Cross nurse called Diane Ryding under the heading 'The Angel and the Agony'. Ryding said later, again to the *Guardian*: 'I don't like it because it is such an untrue image. I get a lot back from my work – I don't do it purely for the love of my fellow man and I am not an angel. Because I am small, blonde and blue-eyed I'm aware I'm being used and that brings the money in.' It was unfortunately the case in 1984 that no one, including the major aid bureaucracies, was prepared to respond properly to the Ethiopian disaster without press

97

coverage of this sort. Ms Ryding continued: 'I appreciate the media do a lot of good, but you do get fed up with the constant stream of cameramen. The people in the camps realize they are getting a lot of attention because they or their children look so ghastly. This is very undignified for them.'

To his credit, Bob Geldof, the Irish pop singer who brought off a series of stunning fund-raising triumphs for famine relief in 1984 and 1985, refused to be photographed holding starving babies. Geldof began by organizing the Band Aid recording of 'Do they know it's Christmas' in Britain; this was followed by the 'USA [United Support of Artists] for Africa' record ' We are the World' in March 1985, and in July those achievements were capped with the Live Aid concert that linked the United States and Britain in sixteen hours of music that was seen in 108 countries. If Western politicians had been relying on what the Americans call 'compassion fatigue' to diminish public interest in the African famine, they were to be disappointed.

The upsurge of public anxiety after the BBC reports caught Governments and international agencies badly off guard. While taking steps to increase their programmes of assistance, some felt the need to defend themselves. In a press release on the subject, the European Community claimed that it 'did not wait for the African famine tragedy to mobilize world public opinion or for the full extent of the catastrophe to be known before taking large-scale emergency action'. Britain's Overseas Development Administration, part of the Foreign Office, responded to public concern by issuing virtually identical press releases three weeks running during November. All began: 'The British Government has responded swiftly to the urgent need for further humanitarian assistance to help the victims of famine in Ethiopia.' All ended in identical terms: 'Britain also took the initiative in stimulating a discussion on the important and difficult task of co-ordinating the efforts of donors in the Committee on Food Aid, the governing body of the World Food Programme.'

When the disquiet over earlier failings had diminished, officials moved on to congratulate themselves on their actions since October. Peter McPherson, head of USAID, was able to declare: 'The American response has been not only significantly faster but also larger than any other donor or institution.' Responding to British concern about how much new aid had been committed, Mrs Thatcher claimed that the British, not the Americans, had been the first to act.

An RAF detachment left Britain to ferry food in Ethiopia on 1 November. The delay of nine days from the first BBC news report was not of British making. Over the weekend of 27–8 October, Mrs Thatcher gave clearance for the Ministry of Defence to provide two transport aircraft, but there was a hitch as the Addis Ababa authorities considered whether they were going to allow a Western air force to operate in Marxist Ethiopia.

In exchanges with Neil Kinnock, leader of the Labour Party, in the House of Commons in July 1985, Mrs Thatcher declared that she was 'extremely proud of the Government's record on aid to Ethiopia and Sudan'. She then underlined the promptness of the British response. 'We were the first to respond, and that is what the Rt Hon. Gentleman cannot stand ... the Rt Hon. Gentleman is well aware that the Government were the first to respond to the need in Ethiopia ...' It was a curious formulation. The British may well have been the first Government to respond to British television pictures, but the needs of Ethiopia had been mounting for months before the mass starvation captured on TV. Furthermore, in the view of most aid experts, the airlifting of grain was an extremely expensive substitute for sending it by road, a course of action that might have been adopted earlier in 1984.

Had the earlier response to Ethiopia's own appeals been adequate, there would have been no need for helter-skelter relief operations. At a development seminar held at the University of Sussex in December 1984, Trevor Page of the World Food Programme described emergency relief operations as 'the last bastion of unprofessionalism'. There were lingering doubts, too, about the motivation of the major donors. Were they finally responding to Ethiopian needs or were they acting because public opinion now demanded that they do something? In his foreword to a fine study of the 1973–4 famine in Ethiopia,* Thomas Hughes, President of the Carnegie Endowment for International Peace in Washington, observed, 'The efforts undertaken in the glare of international press publicity sometimes seem more designed to end the publicity than to aid the afflicted.'

On one matter the Western donors were definite – they had done much better than the Russians. 'Let them eat cement' was the way Peter McPherson of USAID summed up the Soviet attitude towards

---

* Jack Shepherd, *The Politics of Starvation*, Carnegie Endowment for International Peace, Washington DC, 1975.

their Ethiopian ally. Chester Crocker, Assistant Secretary for African Affairs at the State Department, told a Senate hearing in January 1985 of the number of times Americans had been approached in Ethiopia to be thanked for what they were doing. 'We think it is the best of America,' he said, 'and the strongest and most telling response we could make to the years of Soviet arms, Soviet ideology and Soviet indifference to poverty that have dominated Ethiopia.'

The Soviet response to the famine probably owed something to the Western media as well. Moscow could hardly be seen ignoring an event affecting a close ally which the West was beginning so conspicuously to assist. Unlike most donors, the Russians had actually answered the March appeal of the Relief and Rehabilitation Commission with 10,000 tonnes of rice. Timothy Raison, Britain's Aid Minister, pointed out that even India had given ten times this quantity of food aid; he did not add that the Indian donation was five times as great as British food aid to Ethiopia in 1984.

Russian action later in the year came entirely in the form of hardware and military personnel. They sent 300 trucks – with drivers – twelve cargo planes, twenty-four helicopters and no fewer than 500 military personnel. Their work rate in food deliveries did not justify such a huge presence, but they could rely on some inflated accounts of their operation from the Ethiopian leader Colonel Mengistu.

At a press conference in November 1984, Mengistu was asked what the Soviet news agency Tass called a 'provocative' question by an American reporter about Soviet and United States assistance to Ethiopia. 'You cannot compare relief from the USSR and from the USA, they are just incomparable,' he replied. 'The USSR guides itself primarily by the principle of proletarian solidarity ... I can say that three-quarters of deliveries of food and other basic necessities to the disaster-stricken areas and the evacuation of tens of thousands of people are being done by transport made available by the Soviet Union.' That was far from being the whole truth. There was virtually no Soviet food aid to speak of; Soviet aircraft were desperately under-utilized compared with the work rate of, say, the RAF; and while the Russians were certainly responsible for the evacuation of famine victims, that was because Western donors would not participate in what they regarded as an enforced resettlement programme.

That the Russians should be so warmly complimented by Mengistu infuriated American officials. Massive quantities of American food – approaching half the country's aid needs – had done nothing to improve the snarling relationship between the two countries. The number of staff at the US Embassy in Addis Ababa had been pegged by the Ethiopians to only twenty-eight, and that included secretaries, communications personnel and Marine Corps guards. In response to projected levels of American aid, they were allowed five more on temporary attachment. 'That's what we get for giving them $250,000 million in a year – four staffers and another secretary,' a senior diplomat told me in disgust. 'We were faced with a moral dilemma. Should we support a Government that blatantly ignores human rights, yet how can we sacrifice women and children for a political cause? The decision we've made was politically stupid, but morally correct.'

Public agitation in the West can hardly have been the reason for Ethiopia's own leadership finally taking its responsibilities seriously, although the alarm of Western relief agencies in the country played a big part. A meeting of the Politburo on 3 October, some three weeks after the tenth anniversary celebrations, finally gave priority to what was simply called 'the drought'. Each member of the Politburo was allocated a task in the emergency operation. The famine now became 'official', and that enabled journalists to travel once again to the North. There remained, however, a reluctance on the part of the leadership to admit to the full gravity of the situation. The Politburo was reported to have given priority to the 'drought problem which had severely affected the major part of the African Continent due to changes in climatic conditions in recent years', and then to have 'discussed in detail the drought conditions in Ethiopia'.

Only in 1985 did the régime adopt measures that acknowledged the enormity of the crisis confronting the country. On 9 February, Mengistu addressed the nation on a radio and television broadcast. As well he might, he recalled that mass starvation in the North had been one of the major factors behind the revolution in 1974. He was now demanding that every Ethiopian contribute one month's pay as a 'famine levy'. For farmers, that became 100 kilos of grain. Luxury imports, primarily cars and textiles, were to be banned. There was to be strict petrol rationing that limited private car users to about three gallons a week, and private cars were also to be off the roads from dawn to midnight on Sundays. Finally, all Ethiopians were to be available for work in the new resettlement camps by which the Government set great store as a long-term solution to famine in the North.

For much of 1985, the *Ethiopian Herald* carried an inspiring little slogan at the top of the front page. 'We shall overcome hunger through hard work,' it said. At least the leadership itself was now treating the famine with some seriousness.

As well as big aid shipments from the West after October 1984, there was also a succession of visitors to Ethiopia. They were termed simply 'known personalities' by the Ethiopian press. There were Cardinals and pop singers and actors and many leading United Nations figures and even more Western politicians. Among the latter was Senator Edward Kennedy with his daughter Kara and his son Teddy. They spent Christmas 1984 in the camps. In an article he wrote for *People* magazine, Kennedy wondered, 'Are we grandstanding by coming here?' and then answered his own question: 'I don't think so.' Unlike Geldof, but like so many other politicians, he could not resist being photographed with a starving child.

Kennedy quoted his son as saying: 'It's all so preventable, so senseless. To come from the United States and to see so many children dying of starvation, it makes me feel so angry and helpless. It's so unfair and wrong.' As a leading proponent of Third World causes, the Senator might have recalled his own querying of the United States response to the last great Ethiopian famine in 1973–4 when America's imperial ally Haile Selassie was still on his throne. At a Senate hearing in March 1974 he questioned a senior USAID official: 'Is not the real reason for our slow response that we just did not want to blow the whistle on the Ethiopian Government? ... As a result, a lot of people starved to death.' The USAID official replied: 'There was [a] feeling among many of the donor groups that raising this to too public an issue, embarrassing the Government, could in fact harm the kind of co-operation we see as needed on their part. In that sense, perhaps the whistle was not blown loudly enough.' A decade later thousands more Ethiopian people were starving to death. The régime had changed, a different set of circumstances had dictated American inaction, but still the richest nation in the world had failed by timely intervention to prevent one of the world's greatest disasters.

9

Flights to Where?

It was possible to hear the Hercules long before you saw it. In the Ethiopian highlands, in the middle of the wet season, clouds boil up from deep canyons to obscure the peaks and ridges; it makes for treacherous flying. The flight that morning to the hill-top village of Rabel had already been delayed for two hours to allow the sun to burn off some of the cloud, but now the Hercules was somewhere overhead with its cargo of 16 tonnes of grain. A crowd of several hundred villagers had gathered to watch in awed silence as Operation Tesfa – Operation Hope – chalked up another mission.

First, the RAF ground party ignited a smoke flare so the pilot could confirm wind direction. Then came a dry run over the drop-zone; and then it was for real. The Hercules roared in at a height of 25 feet above the ground, and at a word of command from the flight deck a final heave from the men in the belly of the aircraft sent several tonnes of grain toppling to earth. This was the 'heavy free drop' technique in action. The grain is secured on wooden pallets and double-bagged to limit spillage on impact. Even then, as the pallets crashed to the ground and the bags bowled along the drop-zone, several burst open and the grain cascaded away. But this was Ethiopia in the famine, and nothing would be wasted; every single grain was retrieved.

Operation Tesfa began life as Operation Saint Bernard at the beginning of 1985. It was the brainwave of a senior United Nations official posted to Addis Ababa for the emergency. He built on the RAF's experience of food drops in Nepal to construct a truly international operation. Canada was to provide the food and the United Nations to find the bags; the Luftwaffe and the RAF were to provide the aircraft and the daredevil flying; and the Soviet and Polish Air Forces were to provide the helicopters to reconnoitre the drop-zones and take Italian medical teams to the villages.

But the Soviet commander was worried. 'Operation Saint Bernard?'

he asked of the United Nations. 'You are using the name of a Christian saint?' 'No, no, it is the name of a dog,' he was assured. But he was not convinced. Moscow had to be consulted, and Moscow was very worried at the idea of foreigners, Westerners at that, flying on board Soviet helicopters. At the last moment, the Russians pulled out, doing very little for their reputation for philanthropy among Ethiopian relief officials. Along with a Swiss relief agency helicopter, the Polish Air Force took on the role, and delightedly flew anyone who asked to be flown on their Russian-made helicopters – including Western air force personnel, Western Government Ministers and Western journalists.

In the first six months of Operation Tesfa – as it was more neutrally renamed in deference to Communist sensibilities – the RAF dropped 7,000 tonnes of food in areas of the Ethiopian highlands inaccessible by road. The RAF, it was said, reached places that other means of transport could not reach. By the more conventional method of landing with the food, the two Hercules operating in Ethiopia had hauled another 12,000 tonnes of grain by the summer of 1985. And what was said of them by British Ministers was perfectly true: that their reputation in Ethiopia was very high indeed. Their dedication to the job was disconcerting at times. The detachment commander was indignant at a suggestion from the British Ambassador in Addis Ababa that they take Christmas Day off, and a compromise was struck by which they flew on Christmas morning and relaxed for the rest of the day.

The British are good at disasters. With slender resources and in limited theatres, they are probably without equal. Certainly Britain's official case for having responded adequately to the Ethiopian tragedy rests wholly on its disaster services. The RAF outperformed other air forces in the friendly and not-so-friendly rivalries that characterized the international air operations in Ethiopia after October 1984, and at the Overseas Development Administration in London, the redoubtable Miss Dorothy Cherry, head of the Disaster Unit, kept the home fires burning.

Miss Cherry has a firm handshake and an imposing manner. It is quite possible to imagine her arranging a British response to far-flung disaster by force of personality alone. 'You sit at this desk, and realize how jolly lucky you are,' she says of her work. Her unit is small. When I visited her, there was only one other person, and he was looking forward to a quieter life elsewhere in the ODA. Mainly as a result of famine in Africa, Miss Cherry's Disaster Unit has doubled and redoubled its expenditure. Without reference to anyone, she can authorize expenditure up to £250,000; between £250,000 and £500,000 needs agreement from the Finance Department; and only for expenditure above £500,000 does she have to have Ministerial approval.

The Disaster Unit's standing is confirmed by Britain's voluntary agencies, which are not always complimentary about the ODA. Save the Children, for instance, went on record to say that they 'particularly value the flexibility and speed of decision-making of the ODA Disaster Unit'. In the build-up to mass starvation in Ethiopia, it was Miss Cherry's unit that responded. It helped, for instance, with a £100,000 grant towards the establishment of the Save the Children Fund feeding centre in Korem; it supplied Land Rovers both to SCF and to Oxfam, and chipped in to other charities at the time of the first famine appeals.

Even after the explosion of public interest in the famine in October 1984, it was often the small things that counted. In November the British Embassy in Addis Ababa learnt that machines which bagged the relief grain at the port of Assab were idle because the heavy-duty needles had all broken. A telegram was sent to the Foreign Office, and was handled by the ODA's Disaster Unit. Within a day the Crown Agents who are responsible for procuring such things had located the needles, and they were despatched to Addis Ababa by very heavy diplomatic bag. The RAF then flew them on to Assab, and the bagging machines were working again within 48 hours of the original request. The needles cost the British Government less than £300.

The initials ODA stand, however, not for Overseas Disasters Administration, but for Overseas Development Administration. Its budget for the financial year from April 1984, which embraced six months of enhanced commitment to famine in Africa, was £1.1 billion. Miss Cherry's share of that was £12.3 million, just over one-hundredth of the total. The special Joint Funding Scheme by which ODA channels development funds through voluntary agencies accounted for £3.6 million, say one-three-hundredth of the total. The real issues surrounding Britain's official response to the famine have accordingly very little to do with the effectiveness of these tiny operations.

When the RAF arrived in Ethiopia in November 1984, the British committed themselves to a three-month operation. Because Mrs

Thatcher herself was eager to make the gesture, and because senior RAF officers appreciated that it was good training, the Ministry of Defence agreed to pick up the bill. And at £1.5 million a month, the RAF did not come cheap. At the beginning of 1985, their tour of duty was extended, and then in June it was announced that the aircraft would be withdrawn in September. Ethiopian relief officials never wanted them to leave; Church leaders in Britain appealed to Mrs Thatcher to keep them flying; and, moreover, hugely successful fund-raising exercises like the Live Aid concert in July maintained unexpected pressure on the Government. The result was a tactical withdrawal by Timothy Raison, Britain's Minister for Overseas Development, and the RAF operation was extended until December.

Since February, the cost of keeping the RAF airborne in Ethiopia had been shared between the Overseas Development Administration and the Ministry of Defence. By the end of June the Defence share was put at £8.25 million; by December it would be around £12 million. These were important figures because they represented the only additional expenditure sanctioned by the British Government during the entire famine emergency. The rest of the cost of the RAF operation fell on an Overseas Development budget that had been fixed in 1983. 'The RAF is doing a spectacular job,' said Hugh Goyder, Oxfam field director in Ethiopia throughout the emergency, 'but if it means that they are eating into the development budget, then I am afraid that I am opposed to them.'

The issue of 'new' money for the African emergency begged some questions about the priorities behind the Thatcher Government's budgetary restraint. The Treasury's own Contingency Reserve could be utilized for such national crises as the Falklands War or the miners' strike, but the African famine was firmly not in that category. 'It is an inescapable fact of Government that one has a budget,' declared Timothy Raison. It was a view that even some leading Conservatives rejected, a rejection forcefully articulated by the former Prime Minister Edward Heath. 'In the past we have never said on the occasion of a disaster that our contribution to aid must come out of our normal contributions for ordinary purposes,' Heath told the House of Commons in October 1984. 'I hope that such a view will never be accepted by my colleagues on the Government Front Bench. If there is a disaster, additional money must be made available.'

The Conservative-majority Foreign Affairs Committee of the

House of Commons came to the same conclusion in their report 'Famine in Africa', published in May 1985. They asserted that 'the generosity of the British public has not been matched by the British Government'. The report went on: 'We consider that it is not acceptable that almost the entire costs of the UK response to the crisis should fall on the previously agreed ODA budget. The emergency is of such a degree that it must be regarded as a new situation and substantial new money should be provided to help with it.'

Having got very little change out of the Government on the subject, the Committee returned to the attack in a further report on Britain's overseas expenditure in June. 'We repeat our previous conclusion that it is important that the emergency support for famine in Africa should not reduce the money devoted to development,' the Committee stated. 'We believe that the aid budget should be compensated at least by the amount spent on emergency relief in Sub-Saharan Africa which in the year 1984/85 was in the order of £95 million.'

Before an audience untutored in where Britain's aid budget was suffering and how, Timothy Raison could afford a flourish of rhetoric to obscure the point. At a United Nations conference on the famine in Geneva in March 1985, he said: 'The last months have shown that you can count on the generosity of the British people; you can also count on the response of their Government.' Even with the subtle distinction between public 'generosity' and Governmental 'response', it was not a line that could be easily sustained for a critical home audience. In the House of Commons he elaborated upon his view that it was for public opinion to dictate Government response, rather than for Government to initiate action. 'As we know, the public have responded with great generosity,' he said on 11 June. 'If people feel that more should be spent, this is an area where they can do exactly what they feel, through our admirable voluntary agencies.' It was a fine expression of the Thatcherite philosophy that taxpayers should be free to spend their income as they wished. It could, however, be challenged: first, starvation involved a set of moral imperatives for everyone, including officialdom; and second, long-term solutions to Africa's problems could only be pursued with decisive intervention by Western Governments.

The fact that Britain's aid budget had not been increased to accommodate extra expenditure in Africa meant that other parts of Britain's aid programme suffered. What members of the Foreign

107

Affairs Committee found so frustrating was that they were unable to pinpoint exactly which parts these were. For a time, the Government argued that the additional expenditure could be managed within the ODA's contingency reserve which the Treasury helpfully disclosed to be £55 million for the year. But when the Government's own figures for assistance to Africa climbed well above £55 million – some £54 million on its own account and £40 million through the EEC – this line of defence crumbled. The Foreign Affairs Committee was then told that the money had been found from the contingency reserve and 'slippages' in the regular programme. There were apparently regular 'underspends' in the overseas aid budget, and this was where the extra money had come from.

As a matter of policy, ODA does not say what it intends to spend in particular countries or on particular programmes until the money has been spent. It was even irritated with the Treasury for telling the world how much it had in reserve. What was plain, however, was that it never returned an 'underspend' to the Treasury at the end of the year, so someone, somewhere, was losing out. In evidence to the Foreign Affairs Committee, a senior official in the ODA's Africa Division was asked whether, in the absence of a famine emergency, ODA would have spent both its contingency reserve and any other money it had available. 'Yes, that must be so,' the official replied, 'because obviously we are obliged to spend the aid programme every year in accordance with Ministerial policy. Whether it would have gone to development aid as such, or to organizations which deal with emergencies such as UNHCR [United Nations High Commissioner for Refugees], obviously I cannot say.' At the end of the day, the Committee simply recorded that Ministers had been 'able to evade direct questions on the subject'.

The Commons committee also cast a sceptical eye over some of the ODA's public relations footwork. At issue again was the matter of 'new' money. On 23 November 1984, ODA issued a press release headlined 'More Aid for African Drought Relief'. The gullible might have assumed that the Government was digging deep to help Africa, an impression perhaps strengthened by the opening paragraph of the release: 'Mr Timothy Raison, MP, Minister for Overseas Development, has approved a further £1.7 million for emergency aid for victims of drought in Sudan, Chad, Ethiopia, Somalia and the Central African Republic.' The money was being channelled through the worthiest possible agencies: Save the Children Fund, Oxfam, the League of Red Cross Societies, and the United Nations High Commissioner for Refugees.

What the Committee wanted to know was whether this was 'further' in the dictionary sense of additional or whether this was part of the £5 million already announced in October as the British contribution to famine relief. 'A part of it was further and part of it was implementation of the £5 million,' the Minister told the Committee, 'so it was further in the sense that it was new information – but part of it, as I say, came out of the £5 million.' But was the other part of it still 'further'? Raison had to write to the Committee to clear the matter up in December 1984. 'These sums for Sudan and Chad were in fact part of the £5 million and other items in the Press Notice were similarly new allocations but from other existing commitments. The notice was thus about further allocations rather than further commitments.' So at last the truth was out: none of it was 'further'!

The Conservatives had been in power for five years when the African famine emergency became a national issue. In the year Mrs Thatcher won the election, Britain's commitment to overseas aid stood at 0.52 per cent of Gross National Product, some 0.2 per cent off the target set by the United Nations General Assembly at the start of what was supposed to be the Second Development Decade in 1971. Since then, it had slipped and kept on slipping. In 1984, overseas aid accounted for 0.33 per cent of GNP, less than half the UN target.

The value of British aid to the Third World also fell steadily during the first five Thatcher years. The Conservative-majority Foreign Affairs Committee said that British aid had been cut by 7.7 per cent since 1979 compared with an 11 per cent increase during the last Labour Government and a 6 per cent increase during the Heath Government of the early 1970s. Taking inflation into account, the real cut in British aid under Mrs Thatcher was around 18 per cent. 'As is well known,' said the Committee, 'the reasons for this lie in domestic public expenditure policy rather than any appreciation that extra funds could not be put to good use ...'

A declining aid budget was accompanied by a new hard-faced attitude towards the spending of taxpayers' money in the developing world. And there was nothing apologetic in the new outlook. 'We are out to help the poorest countries, largely in the Commonwealth,' said Timothy Raison in the ODA's 1983 annual report, 'but we are keen to do so with an eye to effectiveness (not always easy in the poorest countries) and also with an eye to British political and commercial interests.' This meant a diminished commitment to multilateral aid channels like the United Nations and more emphasis on the spin-off for British industry and British jobs of the aid programme. Raison stuck firmly to his guns during the months of public and political agitation over the famine. 'My position is clear,' he told the House of Commons in June 1985. 'As I have said, it is right that we should look to British interests, and it is right that the bulk of our bilateral aid should be tied.'

A few weeks after the BBC News coverage of starvation in Ethiopia, there was a more precise threat to the British aid budget. The Treasury wanted cuts in the Foreign and Commonwealth Office budget for 1985, and the FCO was looking to its most substantial component, the aid programme, to provide them. Twenty to thirty million pounds was to be lopped off the £1,130 million that had figured in previous public expenditure estimates. A judicious 'leak' of what was being proposed – the stories suggested a cut of as much as £160 million – and the Government had that unique event, a Conservative revolt on aid, on its hands. For the first time in twenty years, Britain's overseas aid programme had come to the centre of the political stage, and for the first time ever, Conservative backbenchers responding to constituents' concerns had put it there. The idea of an extra cut was quietly dropped.

That was not quite the end of the story. Ministers claimed a small percentage increase in the 1985 aid budget, but that was in cash terms before taking inflation into account. Raison was tackled on the subject in the House of Commons in November, and MPs distinctly heard him make the fateful admission that in real terms it amounted to a cut. The *Hansard* record seems to have saved him from this embarrassing acknowledgement. 'The increase that is represented is about three per cent,' the Minister said. 'That is the increase in cash terms. It may be a *calculation*. It depends on the rate of inflation.' Readers of *Hansard*'s fine print were invited to work out what on earth 'calculation' might have meant here; 'cut' would certainly have made more sense.

On the morning that I watched the RAF's airdrop of grain, I spoke through an interpreter to the local villagers. Intelligent and thoughtful people, they were naturally relieved that there would be enough food to keep their families fed for the next few months, but they were still extremely worried about the future. During the last two famine years they had sold their draught animals and very often their farm implements to make ends meet. Worse, in the current season of starvation, they had eaten all their seed to keep alive. According to a Baptist missionary worker in the village, only a quarter of the local farmers had seed to plant during the rains.

Desperate situations required desperate remedies. Farmers told me that they would try to sow some of the relief grain that the RAF was about to drop. I could find no one who could give me a definite answer as to whether this would yield anything at all. But even if the grain had not been chemically treated to prevent germination, it was very doubtful that Canadian wheat from the prairies would flourish at altitude in the soil of the Ethiopian highlands. It is here that an important distinction is employed by donors from the rich world. 'Relief' means the food that the West gives away to keep people alive. Everyone says that is a good thing. Seeds, oxen and farm implements are regarded by some as part of 'development', and a different set of rules applies. Like the provision of clean water, basic irrigation or training in more advanced agriculture, these inputs are of more general benefit. They promote self-sufficiency; they may even help the national economy; they are accordingly frowned upon by some donors.

To read their public observations, it would be assumed that British officials were anxious to promote self-sufficiency in Ethiopia. Time and time again in interviews towards the end of 1984, Timothy Raison stressed that the answer to Africa's problems lay in development, not emergency aid. On my own programme *TV Eye* in early November he stated: 'We all know what really matters is the longer-term development aid. In a way, that's what my Department is about. We have to do the short-term. We're a little bit fearful that the short-term will push us off the long-term. We have to find ways of making sure that the potential food production of Africa, which is enormous, is realized.'

In words if not in deeds, such an approach had been approved at the highest level. In June 1984, before the Ethiopian emergency became a national issue, Mrs Thatcher played hostess in London to the annual economic summit of Western heads of Government. 'We are greatly concerned about the acute problems of poverty and drought in parts of Africa,' the communiqué said, and stated that heads of Government

111

had agreed 'to maintain and wherever possible increase flows of resources, including official development assistance and assistance through the international financial and development institutions, to the developing countries and particularly to the poorest countries ...' As we have already seen from British aid figures, this was not a commitment that Mrs Thatcher felt under much of an obligation to honour, but piety was not replaced with hard thought on the issue until much later in the year.

Questioned in the House of Commons in November about Britain's flagging aid budget, Mrs Thatcher was precision itself: 'There will be no question but that we shall be able to respond in the future with humanitarian aid in the same way as we have just responded to Ethiopia.' There were no references to maintaining and wherever possible increasing British aid flows; the word 'development' never passed the Prime Minister's lips. She then reinforced the point: 'The budget in future for the Foreign Office will be quite sufficient to permit humanitarian aid of that kind in future.' As far as Ethiopia was concerned, it was the Prime Minister's view that prevailed. Britain would help keep Ethiopians alive, and nothing more.

Among senior officials at the Overseas Development Administration, including its permanent secretary Sir Crispin Tickell, there is pronounced hostility towards Ethiopia. Scepticism towards Ethiopian economic policies is certainly justified. A lack of incentives for farmers combined with all the rigidities of an over-centralized system has limited the country's capacity to contribute to a resolution of its own problems. But British official antagonism goes further. There are allegations of corruption when by African standards the Ethiopian administration is notably uncorrupt; it is said that there is incompetence when, again by African standards, the administration is fairly efficient. British officials also express the same concern as their American counterparts over Ethiopia's relationship with the Soviet Union, and urge that Western help is in danger of propping up an unrepresentative Marxist régime. 'Fungibility, old boy!' is the ubiquitous caveat; it comes perilously close to straightforward ideological opposition.

I suspect that Timothy Raison became more sympathetic towards Ethiopia as the crisis wore on. After a strained first meeting in late 1983 with Commissioner Dawit of the Relief and Rehabilitation Commission – Raison was briefed by civil servants to chastise him over the alleged misappropriation of food aid – their relationship developed more positively. Raison paid several visits to the country in 1984 and 1985 and went further than many Western Ministers in an understanding of Ethiopia's security problems. According to Dawit, the two men were able to discuss Ethiopia's development problems in detail, even if Britain was not a significant contributor. Raison was certainly more charitably disposed towards Ethiopia than his Conservative predecessor as Minister for Overseas Development, Sir Neil Marten. Marten used to complain at having to make even emergency humanitarian aid available to Ethiopia.

When television pictures placed Ethiopia in the British popular consciousness in autumn 1984, relations between the two Governments were easier than they had been at any time since the revolution. In April 1984, agreement had finally been reached over compensation for the British company Mitchell Cotts, whose cotton plantations had been nationalized in 1975. Negotiations had continued for three years with officials from Ethiopia's Compensation Commission and, in the words of a Mitchell Cotts executive, the company had 'swallowed our ambition' to accept £2.5 million from an original claim of almost £7 million. On the British side, ODA had in 1984 already announced the writing off of some outstanding development loans to Ethiopia.

But even after his first visit to Ethiopia in November, Raison stuck to the Government's view that there should be no development aid. He offered various reasons. A British worker had been shot before the aid programme had been closed down in the 1970s. But that had been during a period of unusual unrest even by Ethiopian standards; no one would expect British aid personnel to go to work now in insecure areas; and the Government seemed to have no reservations in encouraging voluntary agencies to operate with expatriate personnnel in Ethiopia. There was next the question of Ethiopia's attachment to a centralized socialist approach to agriculture, but it seemed to its critics that the ODA was making no effort to look for projects that would circumvent the system to bring benefits to the people. Raison got nearer the mark when he spelt out that Britain was already providing development assistance to more than 120 countries, and that it was reasonable to concentrate on Commonwealth countries. 'I've said before that we should be giving more readily to our friends than our enemies,' the Minister said. Whether the grounds were primarily practical or political, there was going to be no substantial British development programme in Ethiopia.

Raison and his officials were not budged by a persuasive Oxfam paper entitled 'Ethiopia – a Case for British Aid' presented to the ODA in April 1985 at a time when the matter was under active discussion. Oxfam sought to answer the Government's political objections to assisting Ethiopia. 'It is clear that the British Government has no wish to support the present régime's Soviet-style administration such as the centrally planned approach of State farms,' the paper said, but then argued that it would be possible to help Ethiopia's poor in uncontroversial ways. 'After all, 90 per cent of cultivated land in Ethiopia is farmed by peasant farmers, not by State farm authorities.'

Oxfam identified agricultural co-operatives, small-scale irrigation, reafforestation works, and soil and water conservation as areas where British assistance would not involve the endorsement of a Marxist régime. On agricultural co-operatives, even the Minister ruefully acknowledged that Britain had its Milk Marketing Board. 'Oxfam is convinced that this type of aid could help avert famine in the future, would not significantly strengthen the power base of the Ethiopian Government, would not "aid and abet" policies which HMG disagrees with, but *would* be exactly the type of aid programme that the British taxpayer wants to see,' the Oxfam paper concluded.

It is said that Oxfam's arguments received the backing of the British Embassy in Addis Ababa – hardly surprising since diplomats there had lived through the Ethiopian catastrophe – and that there were voices raised in favour within the Foreign Office. Oxfam underlined an argument that would have appealed to the strategists: that there would be a political spin-off from economic support. The enticement of Mozambique from its Marxist moorings owed something to Western aid at a time of severe famine. 'If we abdicate our responsibility and turn a cold shoulder,' said the Oxfam paper, 'then such a policy certainly will isolate Ethiopia from the Western world and push her more and more firmly into the Soviet camp.' Whether from the Minister's own inclinations or as a result of the 'Yes, Minister' blandishments of his senior officials, the Oxfam paper got nowhere. Britain would not start its own development programme in Ethiopia.

Western donors which have started development programmes in Ethiopia say they have managed to maintain them without endorsing Marxism. A Canadian water-resources project in southern Ethiopia, for instance, owed much to British work in the same field which was halted in the late 1970s. 'I've seen our project with my own eyes,' a Canadian diplomat told me in Addis Ababa, 'and I know it works. We're talking about the sort of project that no political system can screw up.'

The British have been equally unforthcoming in their response to United Nations appeals for development funds for Ethiopia. Politics may here have been allied to the prosaic matter of money, with the failure to commit more funds to the African emergency inhibiting further contributions. UNICEF, the United Nations Children's Fund, has an effective programme in Ethiopia, and in 1985 launched an appeal for a further $35 million. The British did not contribute. The UN's Food and Agriculture Programme held a meeting in Rome in January 1985 at which twenty agricultural projects were presented to donors. Again, the British did not contribute.

At the London economic summit in June 1984, Mrs Thatcher and her fellow heads of Government declared their warm support for an important World Bank initiative for Africa. The communiqué stated: 'We attach major importance to the special action programme for Africa which is being prepared by the World Bank and should provide renewed impetus to the joint efforts of the international community to help.' This was largely flannel, at least on the part of Britain and the United States. So marked was their lack of enthusiasm that the new fund's original target of $2 billion was reduced to $1.25 billion.

The United States declined to contribute at all to the fund, preferring to launch its own Economic Policy Initiative for Africa, intended to encourage African states more robustly than even the World Bank along the path of free-market righteousness. The Bank commented: 'It is Bank management's hope that the US, at some future date, will participate in the Facility.' The British had no ideological difficulties with the fund since it could be applied throughout black Africa, but ODA's response was nevertheless peculiarly convoluted. Instead of contributing direct, the Government agreed to commit money to Africa on the same terms as the World Bank. It then took several months of negotiations for the British to agree that their contributions need not be tied exclusively to British goods and services. Japan contributed $300 million to the fund; France and Italy provided $150 million each; the British managed just £15 million a year for five years.

In denying development assistance to Ethiopia, Britain was following closely in the footsteps of the United States. Unlike the British Government, however, which could make up the rules as it went along, the Reagan Administration owed a debt to two former Senators, one of them dead, who had already delineated the rules for them. The late Senator Bourke Hickenlooper of Iowa had been so outraged when the Brazilians nationalized American property that, in 1962, he promoted an amendment to the Foreign Assistance Act declaring that it was no longer legal to provide development assistance to a country that had nationalized American property without compensation. So the fact that the Kalamazoo Spice Company of Michigan was not yet satisfied with the terms offered by Ethiopia's Compensation Commission meant that the Administration could invoke 'Hickenlooper' to deny the country development aid.

If 'Hickenlooper' did not apply, there was always 'Brooke'. Senator Edward Brooke of Massachusetts was responsible for an amendment to the Foreign Assistance Act stipulating that no country could receive development aid which had failed to pay instalments on loans for military purchases. American military hardware had continued to be delivered to Ethiopia even after the revolution, but the new régime had defaulted on repayments. No repayments, no development aid. In the months of growing US food aid commitments to Ethiopia after October 1984, Brooke and Hickenlooper were honoured to the letter. Towards the end of 1984, USAID refused to buy seed for the American Save the Children Fund to distribute in the famine zone, and it turned down a similar request early in 1985 that would have allowed the Ethiopian Government to acquire US relief grain for feeding city dwellers so that it could transfer its own seed to the countryside.

The American press did much to highlight the workings of Hickenlooper and Brooke, and once again in response to such pressure the Administration gave ground. The Hickenlooper amendment had already been specifically waived by Congress in the additional funds it voted in April 1985, and in a telegram to the United States Embassy on 8 May, it was spelt out that new aid could finance 'relief, rehabilitation and recovery projects, including the provision of seeds for planting, fertilizer, pesticide, farm implements, farm animals, vaccines ...' The list was a long one.

When I visited Ethiopia in June 1985, this liberalized policy was bearing modest fruit. The United States was providing 2,500 tonnes of wheat to the International Committee of the Red Cross so that the ICRC could pass on seed to farmers. But it was a tiny amount and it was also very late. The sowing season began along with the rains in June. Had there been an earlier commitment to enable Ethiopia to recover from the ravages of famine, decisions on basic inputs like seeds would have been taken in good time for the planting season.

The British Government decided to provide no seed at all. This would be left, said Ministers, to the European Community to whose aid budget the British contributed. It was one of the more ironic aspects of the British response to the African emergency that politicians were content both to be outspokenly critical of the European Community's operations and yet pick up any credit for its programme. This was duly noted in Brussels. 'The only thing that has increased from Britain during this famine is the level of criticism directed at us,' one Commission official growled at me.

However, the Government inched towards other programmes in what had originally been regarded as the development field. In April 1985, an order was placed for £54,000 worth of spades and hoes for distribution among farmers who had lost or sold their implements. The idea was that they should arrive in time for the rains in June, but they did not. In autumn 1985, the first students in many years to be nominated by the Ethiopian Government arrived in Britain. Their courses would include agriculture. This was an encouraging sign for Ethiopia. The only Ethiopians on courses in Britain until that time had been Eritreans and Tigreans from the rebel areas, and in a bizarre bit of handiwork they had gone down in the published statistics as official British aid to Ethiopia.

Perhaps the implicit distinction drawn by Mrs Thatcher in November 1984 between 'humanitarian' and 'development' aid was beginning at last to break down. Seen from the Ethiopian countryside, it made little sense. As Dawit Wolde Giorgis of the Relief Commission expressed it in December 1984: 'There is nothing more humanitarian, in our minds, than to give people constantly affected by drought the chance to lead peaceful, productive lives in which their labour will not be wasted by the vagaries of nature, and in which they will not need to remain dependent, year after year, on relief hand-outs from the Commission.'

It was an argument that would have been echoed by the American

117

relief official who was quoted in May 1985 complaining about the restrictions placed on US food aid. 'We can only give American food to people sitting on their ass,' he said. 'You keep people alive only to starve.'

10

A Divided Family

If a United Nations committee ever sat down to design the perfect UN bureaucrat, it would end up inventing Kurt Jansson. Tall, lean, grey-haired, punctilious in manner, soberly suited, speaking perfect English with an understated foreign accent and with a name that narrows his origins down to one of a number of acceptable northern European states, Jansson could hardly be improved upon. Such credentials kept him at work long after his retirement in 1977.

In 1980 he was called upon to run the United Nations operation in Kampuchea. Then, in November 1984, at the age of 69, he was appointed Assistant Secretary General for Emergency Operations in Ethiopia. His success in the position provided a fine climax to a career of international service that began in his native Finland after World War II. His job then had been the resettlement of refugees from Karelia in the aftermath of the Russo-Finnish war. The plight of the Karelians – thrust backwards and forwards during the years of conflict – had distant echoes with the distress of refugees in the marches of the Ethiopian empire, now also a modern Communist state.

Jansson and his team were given a corner of the sixth floor of the United Nations building in Addis Ababa. Apart from some hastily rigged telephones, there was nothing but his calm assurance to guarantee that the job would be done. In contrast to some other United Nations offices in the building – brittle secretaries and self-important bosses – there was a good-natured and efficient hum to the Jansson operation. It owed much to the unflagging charm of Suman Dhar, secretary and administrative assistant to Jansson who had served him in Kampuchea and had once again been plucked from her UNICEF office in New Delhi.

Jansson's task was to get the food through. The UN's earlier predictions about Ethiopia's limited port capacity proved unfounded; with some new handling equipment there would be no difficulty

119

bringing in the million tonnes required for the twelve months of the Jansson operation. Distribution within Ethiopia was a bigger problem. 'The world has a 300 million tonne surplus of food, so there is no difficulty raising one million tonnes,' Jansson told me. 'But the world has no surplus of trucks.' For the six months from December 1984 to May 1985, food was being distributed at a rate of 45,000 tonnes a month, more than four times what the United Nations had previously judged to be possible. Part of this was doubtless due to Jansson himself; part to the enhanced commitment of the Ethiopian leadership; part to new transport that had begun arriving as aid; but the biggest single reason remained, I suspect, that the UN had got its arithmetic badly wrong in 1984.

The key to Jansson's success was that he gained the respect of everyone in a jungle of competing interests and prejudices. It would probably be overstating the matter to say that he and Colonel Haile Mariam Mengistu, the Ethiopian leader, actually got on well together. The Colonel is not a man to encourage intimacy. But as their meetings continued, Mengistu relaxed in the older man's company and spoke candidly of their mutual problems. Ethiopian relief officials also thought a great deal of Jansson. 'He's doing a very good job,' observed Commissioner Dawit of the RRC, 'considering he's a donor man.' The major donors relied heavily on him; indeed at one remove the United States may have engineered his appointment in the first place. The East bloc countries found an efficient Finn quite acceptable; even the man who had been the fall guy in the Jansson appointment, Dr Kenneth King of the United Nations Development Programme, thought he was doing an excellent job. As an admiring senior UN official remarked of Jansson: 'He's almost too good to be true; the man's an angel.'

The Jansson appointment represented what can best be described as a putsch within the UN system, that agglomeration of warring agencies that is sometimes called a family. In the immediate aftermath of the BBC News film of the famine, Javier Perez de Cuellar, Secretary-General of the United Nations, received an urgent memorandum from two of his most powerful satraps, James Grant, head of UNICEF, and James Ingram, head of the World Food Programme. The burden of the memo was plain: the UN had to be seen to be doing more in Ethiopia. They proposed a new office to run the UN's response to the famine, and they said that Kurt Jansson should run it.

This intervention may have been conceived with the worthiest of motives. But the effect was to upset a United Nations apple-cart. Agencies within the UN system fight for precedence. In bureaucratic jargon, it matters immensely which is the 'lead' agency in a given country, programme or crisis. It matters even more in a high-profile emergency like the Ethiopian famine, where the rewards in terms of budgets and publicity are that much greater.

Perez de Cuellar did more or less as he was asked. Not only was Kurt Jansson appointed to his task, but the appointment was made without any reference to other key players in the United Nations system. In particular, two important figures had been worsted – Bradford Morse, head of the United Nations Development Programme, whose man in Addis Ababa was supposedly the senior UN figure on the scene, and Edouard Saouma, head of the UN's Food and Agriculture Organization. Neither was told in advance of the appointment. Nor incidentally was the Frenchman, Jean Ripert, who holds the lofty title of Director-General of Development in New York and is supposed to be second in command to Perez de Cuellar in all development matters.

But powerful bureaucrats have a way of defending territory. Goodness knows by what process the Secretary-General was persuaded to take his next major decision on the Ethiopian crisis. But six weeks *after* he had appointed Kurt Jansson as his personal representative to co-ordinate the international relief effort in Ethiopia, he created a new office to which he ordered Jansson to report. The man he appointed to head the new office was Bradford Morse, the former Massachusetts Congressman who runs the United Nations Development Programme. I was told that there were several blazing rows over the telephone between New York and Addis Ababa as Morse sought to impose his authority on Jansson. But the important thing was that precedence had been re-established. UNDP was back with its nose in front of UNICEF and the FAO. There was even a name for the new office. It was to be the Office of Emergency Operations in Africa, or OEOA. If UN initials were edible, no one would have gone hungry in Ethiopia.

The significance of Perez de Cuellar's reaction to the Ethiopian

121

emergency went beyond personality. It demonstrated that the UN was no different from more popular institutions when it came to responding to a major televised disaster; that it was almost as important to be seen to be responding as to achieve anything. In making the Jansson appointment and creating a special new office, Perez de Cuellar was downgrading other specialist UN institutions and subordinating other individuals who supposedly had a key role to play in disasters.

Kurt Jansson was critical of aspects of his own appointment to senior colleagues at the United Nations. 'Why is it', he asked them, 'that the response of the UN to every crisis is to create a new office?' He argued that the UN had been 'caught flat-footed' by the wave of public concern over the Ethiopian famine, and that there should be a built-in system of disaster specialization to cope with such crises. In fact, when the Ethiopian emergency arose, the United Nations already had many such bodies and people in the field.

UNDRO (Office of the United Nations Disaster Relief Coordinator) seemed cut out for the Ethiopian emergency. It was established in December 1971, the month that the Indian Army invaded East Pakistan to create independent Bangladesh. The Indian action came after eight months of appalling hardship for Bengali civilians caught between nationalist guerrillas and a ruthless Pakistani administration. There was some hunger, but disease and the sheer misery of being a refugee in the monsoons were worse. With very little administrative assistance from the United Nations, the Indian Government prevented a crisis from becoming a catastrophe. The refugees returned to their liberated homeland. But the UN thought a special organization should be established to help cope with future disasters.

UNDRO was to 'mobilize, direct and co-ordinate the relief activities of the UN system and to co-ordinate the assistance with that given by other inter-governmental and non-governmental organizations'. That was precisely the job that needed to be done in Ethiopia. A year after its formation the UN General Assembly declared that UNDRO would be 'the central co-ordination to develop concerted relief programmes as a basis for united appeals for funds which UNDRO, in turn, would also be responsible for co-ordinating'. Crucially, this seemed to provide the infant organization with a 'lead' role in disasters.

In the build-up to mass starvation in northern Ethiopia, UNDRO had been issuing regular situation reports via its headquarters in

Geneva to the donor countries and to other UN agencies. The reports also went to all the major embassies in Addis Ababa. They began with 'Information Report Number 1' four days after the Ethiopian appeal for massive help on 30 March 1984. On the basis of RRC figures, the report stated that 5.2 per cent of the population in fourteen regions were affected by drought, a calculation that would have meant that some 1.5 million people faced hardship. It was a silly error on UNDRO's part and had to be corrected in a further telex to donors two weeks later. 'Quote 5.2 per cent unquote should read 5.2 million people in fourteen regions,' said the UNDRO report of 18 April.

As the crisis mounted in the Ethiopian countryside, UNDRO betrayed a certain insouciance in its reporting. As late as 18 September, when something approaching panic was gripping private relief agencies in the field, the UNDRO report acknowledged that 'critical situations' were developing in Tigre and Wollo 'due to less than normal rain during July and August', but declared in a fashion that provided fateful reassurance to donors: 'Main growing season ending September provided almost satisfactory growing conditions in major crop-producing areas ...'

It is probable that the same bureaucratic paralysis that prevented the UN's major agricultural agencies from seeing what was happening also affected UNDRO. In May 1984, the Reverend Arthur Simon, executive director of the United States Christian foundation Bread for the World, visited Ethiopia, and reported on the growing seriousness of the drought. 'No one is quarrelling with the Government's assessment of human need,' he told staff on his return. His report demonstrated how outsiders were already challenging FAO/WFP's complacent estimate that only 120,000 tonnes of food could be brought into the country. 'Is 10,000 tonnes a month the limit of capacity?' Simon asked in his report. 'No one else whom we interviewed thought so.' Simon then relayed a revealing observation from a Dutch official called Rens Hesselmans working for UNDRO in Addis Ababa. Hesselmans noted the immense disparity between what the Ethiopian Government said it needed and the limits on aid shipments effectively imposed by the UN's experts. If the experts were followed, and the Ethiopian Government turned out to be right, Hesselmans observed, 'there is going to be a helluva problem'. The comment would make a good epitaph for the UN's disaster planning in Ethiopia.

UNDRO's problem was that the other UN agencies had never let it grow. In 1984, UNDRO had a world-wide staff – UN professionals and secretaries – of fifty. It might have established itself in the early 1970s during the drought emergency in the Sahel, but it was smothered by the Big Brothers of the UN system. The FAO's Office for Sahelian Relief Operations performed the role allocated to UNDRO during that crisis, and then it transformed its Office for Sahelian Relief Operations into another OSRO – the Office for *Special* Relief Operations. It was this OSRO which was responsible for the seriously misleading assessment report on Ethiopia's food needs researched in February 1984 and published four months later.

By the time the UN got around to creating yet another structure to respond to the Ethiopian emergency, the role of UNDRO was being impatiently denigrated on all sides. A senior official at the World Food Programme told me, 'UNDRO is a post-box, frankly.' Maurice Strong, the experienced Canadian brought in as Executive Co-ordinator of the new Office for Emergency Operations in Africa, put it another way. 'UNDRO is a small organization,' he said. 'It can only cope with normal disasters.' The question of UNDRO's size was begged in a similar fashion by British MPs on the House of Commons Foreign Affairs Committee. Its report 'Famine in Africa', published in May 1985, concluded: 'UNDRO's resources appear to be insufficient to make a major contribution in respect of disasters on the scale of the current African emergency.'

Since 1982, UNDRO had been run by M'Hamed Essaafi, a Tunisian appointed to the job from Perez de Cuellar's personal office in New York. He was under no illusions about the failures of the UN's response to the African emergency. 'In our relief work we are fighting a losing battle,' he was quoted as saying. 'Disaster relief must be continued and developed. But some new aspects – preparedness and prevention – must be added.' It would almost certainly not be the specialists of UNDRO who would be allowed to develop such a new role. Up against the tough men who ran the big UN agencies, Essaafi stood little chance of extending his responsibilities. 'Essaafi has one big problem,' I was told by a senior UN official. 'He is too much of a gentleman.'

The United Nations had, of course, long been aware of the crisis building up in Africa. The appointment of Kurt Jansson and the creation of the Office for Emergency Operations in Africa were by no means the first bureaucratic initiatives taken by the UN Secretary-General. Some eight months before television pictures of the Ethiopian famine made the continent's crisis a matter of international public concern, Perez de Cuellar decided to make his first special appointment. Professor Adebayo Adedeji was already executive secretary of the Economic Commission for Africa, a United Nations body based in Addis Ababa. Now he became the Secretary-General's Special Representative on the African Economic Crisis (this was a formal title) and was given an office in Nairobi, capital of neighbouring Kenya.

But Adedeji ran into the same problems as UNDRO had done – the big boys of the system did not care for competition. The *Economist Development Report*, which monitored some of the twists and turns of the international community in its approach to the African crisis in 1984, reported in April that a special inter-agency committee had had to be established in New York to keep the peace among organizations upset by the new appointment. One result was that Adedeji was barred from raising any funds of his own for projects that he thought important. 'It seems the UN has once more ducked hard choices,' commented the *Economist Development Report* on the meeting. When public anxiety in the West forced another change of tack on the United Nations, Professor Adedeji's appointment was quietly forgotten.

As the new United Nations chief in Addis Ababa, Kurt Jansson was also usurping functions that properly belonged to Dr Kenneth King, head of the United Nations Development Programme in Ethiopia. Here it is necessary to enter another terminological thicket. Dr King's position was Resident Representative for UNDP, but that involved far broader responsibilities. He was also Resident Co-ordinator, which gave him precedence over the heads of other UN missions in the country, and he was the senior representative both of the World Food Programme and UNDRO. In short, in the event of something like a famine in Ethiopia, King was supposed to be king.

Some of the grounds for casting Kenneth King aside may have been quite reasonable; others stained the good name of the United Nations. As happens to diplomats accredited to foreign countries, UN officials sometimes become too committed in the eyes of superiors to their host Governments. Dr King liked Ethiopia, liked Ethiopians, and was well disposed towards the Marxist régime. That alone was enough to promote suspicion on the part of some Western Governments, specifically the United States, which bankrolled the United Nations and its agencies. Although Dr King was very senior in the UN system and had been a Minister in his native Guyana, he may not have had the management capacity that Kurt Jansson was to demonstrate. But he was never given much of an opportunity to test the matter one way or the other. When Jansson set up shop in Addis Ababa at the end of 1984, he had twelve staff; despite the UN's awareness of the crisis, Dr King was not offered any extra staff in all the preceding months. King had a further problem in the eyes of some: he had become part of the furniture in Addis Ababa. Much of Jansson's success lay in his capacity to make fresh demands on the Ethiopian régime.

To United Nations officials in public, the Jansson appointment was simply a matter of 'elevating the level of command'. But was that the whole story? We have already seen how Kenneth King spoke out for Ethiopia against the decision to limit food aid by the UN's own agencies. In the same British television programme he had directed some elliptical criticisms at United Nations official attitudes towards Ethiopia, and was subsequently rapped over the knuckles in New York for having upset 'the donors'. Dr King is Guyanese, a product of the Third World voicing Third World concerns from the capital of a black Marxist state hostile to the United States. He was certainly not a favourite of the American foreign policy establishment, and some senior UN officials have told me that the United States demanded his replacement. Dr King also suffers from another disability in a world where donor prejudices are often translated into UN action. Like Professor Adedeji, who was similarly passed over, Kenneth King is black.

Dr King played a walk-on part in another important bureaucratic episode that disfigured the UN's response to the Ethiopian tragedy in 1984. This was the state of guerrilla warfare that existed between the two UN agencies charged with responsibility for food and agricultural matters and based in the same quarter of Rome, the Food and Agricultural Organization (FAO) and the World Food Programme (WFP). For a period Dr King had been deputy to Edouard Saouma, director general of the FAO, but the working relationship did not last long. During the build-up to the famine emergency in Ethiopia, the two men were scarcely on speaking terms. A senior UN official described them as 'blood enemies'. That personality clash had its impact on UN performance in Ethiopia, but may not have been as significant as the tension between Saouma and James Ingram, Australian head of the World Food Programme.

The FAO inhabits buildings near the Baths of Caracalla in Rome which were once occupied by Mussolini's Ministry of Colonies. There is a very visible link with Ethiopia, which was briefly colonized by the Italians. Plonked outside the FAO is a priceless stela from Axum, ancient capital of Ethiopia, which Mussolini had carted back to Italy and which the Ethiopians would now like returned. A UN bus travels from the FAO past the Baths of Caracalla and through the city walls to the more modern offices of WFP. The regularity of that service has done nothing for good relations between the two organizations.

The World Food Programme is the biggest of the UN's aid-givers after the World Bank. Since 1963, it has provided food aid worth $8 billion. Because food is expensive and bulky, WFP remains a very slender organization by UN standards. It has some 300 professional staff compared with about 7,000 at the FAO. WFP's constitution is a particularly complex piece of United Nations handiwork, and it is this which has led to trouble. When WFP was established, the United States as the world's major food aid donor did not want its bounty falling into the hands of UN bureaucrats who might not be America's friends, so a constitutional truss was devised for the new bird. In certain matters, WFP was its own master; in others it had to defer to the FAO; in still others, like top appointments, a joint responsibility was shared by the FAO and the Secretary-General on the other side of the Atlantic. These areas were always potential theatres of war; it was unfortunate for the hungry of Africa that a struggle for bureaucratic precedence in Rome reached its climax when their interests should have been paramount.

James Ingram, who ran the Australian Government's aid programme before becoming head of WFP, wanted independence for his agency, or at least Dominion status. Saouma wanted to keep WFP where it was; that is, largely under his own thumb. The war was waged over what a UN report itself described as the 'extraordinary overlapping of responsibilities between the two organizations'. According to the FAO, WFP should be content with a role of locating, shipping and monitoring food aid; the FAO would get on with the more complex task of defining need. According to WFP, the FAO could get on with crop assessment; decisions on deficit and aid

127

requirements were clearly for WFP. It was a bureaucrats' delight, and special UN task forces and inspection units were formed in 1984 to conduct detailed inquiries into the matter.

The Joint Inspection Unit of the United Nations, based in Geneva, conducted its inquiries into the relationship between the FAO and WFP early in 1984, and the report was published as deaths from starvation in Ethiopia reached their height in September. Entitled 'Report on WFP Personnel Problems', it was first printed in French and English. But this was the United Nations, so it was then translated into Arabic, Chinese, Russian and Spanish. The report seemed to take WFP's side in the dispute, pointing out that some of its earlier recommendations had not been acted upon. It then detailed the seven stages through which any senior appointment at WFP had to go, a process apparently intended to keep the organization in a harness of the FAO's design. In a crucial observation, the report stated that the necessary links between the FAO and WFP 'have been confused with control of WFP activities by FAO'.

It is one of bureaucracy's fundamental laws that plausible grounds can always be found for never acting on unpalatable conclusions. Instead of implementing the findings of the Joint Inspection Unit, the next stage in November 1984 at the height of international concern over starvation in Africa was to establish a special Task Force of senior officials to look further into the matter. To guarantee the right conclusion, Perez de Cuellar in New York and Saouma in Rome declared in advance that they rejected the inspectors' recommendation that an overhaul of the FAO–WFP relationship was necessary, and told the Task Force to study matters in that light. Certain minor changes were thus authorized, but WFP remained under the FAO's thumb. Perez de Cuellar and Saouma justified this on the grounds that 'food aid is provided in the context of economic and social development, depends on the agricultural situation and availability and in turn affects the food and agricultural economy'. It was an expression of the sound view that stop-gap measures like food aid should always be part of a wider development effort; it was precisely that link which was broken when the Secretary-General appointed Kurt Jansson to run an exclusively emergency operation in Ethiopia in November 1984.

The full extent of the animosity between James Ingram of WFP and Edouard Saouma at the FAO has been hidden from public view. The

128

six-man Task Force established by Perez de Cuellar and Saouma declared that all its documentation would be 'confidential and not disclosed to any unauthorized person or authority'. But it was never a decorous dispute. Much of the argument took place in the Committee on Food Aid Policies and Programmes, which is WFP's governing body and on which fifteen members of the FAO Council sit. At meetings in 1984 this inter-agency row was never far from the surface. I was told that one of the choicer insults hurled by Saouma supporters at Ingram's men was that they were 'monkeys'.

I tried to discuss the importance of this unholy row with senior officials in Rome. There was invariably an embarrassed silence. Fear and loathing in Rome were themselves of little consequence, of course, but was there a sense in which Rome had fiddled while Africa starved? 'To the extent that this matter took up about 30 per cent of the time of the most important officials of both organizations, I am afraid it did have an impact,' a senior official finally and ashamedly told me.

One of the ways in which Edouard Saouma has continued to exercise his control over the operations of the World Food Programme is the authorization that he must give for emergency shipments of food. The procedure is that a formal request has to come from the Government concerned, and that in approving a shipment he takes into account the 'analysis and recommendation' of the Executive Director of WFP, James Ingram. In theory, it should be a very straightforward exercise. The two organizations are within a few miles of each other and all that is really required is a signature. In practice, it often takes no more than a day or two, and the established upper limit is ten days.

In May 1984, Trevor Page, head of emergency services at WFP, toured Ethiopia at a time when there were already 15,000 destitute people in the Save the Children Fund feeding centre in Korem. By any criteria Ethiopia qualified for emergency assistance. On his return to Rome, Page helped Ethiopian officials draw up a request for 26,000 tonnes of food which was then rushed through WFP's own procedures in early June and presented with all the proper recommendations to Saouma for final approval. A week passed and Saouma approved a tiny fraction of this large shipment, 200 tonnes of biscuits. Some of these biscuits were airlifted out of Amsterdam within days and were then rapidly sent on to famine areas in southern Ethiopia. The rest of the biscuits were located in a UN stockpile in Cairo, and naturally

Egyptian bureaucracy had to make its contribution to famine relief; it took until August 1984 for the Egyptians to grant an export licence for the biscuits.

But what of the remaining 25,800 tonnes of emergency food aid presented to Saouma for final clearance? Having received the request on 7 June, he did not put his signature to the papers until 27 June. It was a performance that merited an official protest from WFP. There is little doubt that the delay was deliberate. What remains unclear is why Saouma should have withheld approval for this shipment to Ethiopia. The FAO's Office of Special Relief Operations Report on Ethiopia was finally published in June after a similarly inexplicable delay of three months, and Saouma certainly emphasized to donors the country's incapacity to handle more than 10,000 tonnes a month. But there is no reason to believe that Saouma was prejudiced against Ethiopia itself. Senior officials in other agencies believe that the delay in the emergency shipment may have resulted simply from Saouma's antagonism towards Ingram at WFP and Ingram's senior representative in Addis Ababa, Dr Kenneth King.

If Saouma's position as Director-General of the FAO was dependent on the votes of people and not Governments, he might have left office some years ago. But this Lebanese warlord has brilliantly defended his Roman fiefdom since 1976. Indeed, he has been able to change the rules to extend his term of office, then to seek re-election, and now to look for a third term in 1987. He has managed it by securing the support of Third World Governments, and no bloc has been more important than the African states. The most serious allegation against him is that he stretched the list of African countries affected by drought to the limit in deference more to diplomatic requirements than to the needs of the hungry. Whether true or not, the effect was to distract donors' attention from the relatively few countries where there was a grave danger of widespread starvation.

When it comes to the rhetoric of development, Saouma is a master. On World Food Day, in October 1984, there were a number of special ceremonies and events on the theme of 'Women in Agriculture'. 'We at FAO are constantly intensifying our efforts to ensure that our activities and projects give full consideration and support to the role of women in food production and in the rural community generally,' he told guests in Rome. He might well have subscribed to this ideal for Third World food production, but certainly not in running his own empire. In their inquiry into staffing matters at the FAO and WFP, the UN inspectors found that women of the FAO's professional staff comprised just 10 per cent of the total, one of the lowest of any UN agency.

The attitudes of Edouard Saouma were not the only problem faced by the World Food Programme in trying to mobilize emergency food aid for Ethiopia in the summer of 1984. Having at last received Saouma's authorization, there was next the problem delicately defined by WFP as 'donor identification'. Commitments to the International Emergency Food Reserve, the instrument by which WFP could respond to crises around the world, did not mean that donors had ceased to exercise control over their food aid. As often as not, the problem of 'donor identification' meant persuading the Americans to cough up.

WFP's emergency food reserve had met its target of 500,000 tonnes three years in succession by 1984. But commitments to the reserve and decisions to aid particular countries were different matters. Proposals to make the contributions legally binding on donors had been resisted by major food aid providers like the United States and the European Community precisely because, it was said, this would give additional power and influence to Saouma in Rome. 'As a result,' said an internal WFP review of emergency food aid deliveries in May 1985, 'some operations may not be approved promptly while others, perhaps of lesser importance, will be accepted because of the availability of supplies in the overall food basket.'

In June 1984, the United States was still not looking for opportunities to help Ethiopia. Some 8,000 tonnes of wheat and quantities of high-energy supplementary foods were eventually to come from the United States, but for an urgent response WFP had to look elsewhere. Sweden made a contribution of 10,000 tonnes towards the total approved in Rome, and that arrived in Ethiopia in September, extremely fast by UN standards. According to WFP records, the consignment in its entirety was not so prompt. By the end of the year, 9,000 of the 26,000 tonnes approved still had to be distributed. In its review of emergency operations, WFP found that the average time between the request and delivery of urgent food was five months. Although WFP was managing to shave valuable days off this time, delivery in a quarter of cases examined in 1983–4 had been 'unduly slow' and taken more than seven months. So firm were the constraints on the International Emergency Food Reserve that emergency shipments sometimes took *longer* than the even more cumbersome regular food aid shipments.

Despite a mediocre performance in 1984, the World Food Programme emerged later in 1985 as one of the few UN agencies to have enhanced its reputation during the African emergency. A special secretariat was established in its transport branch at the beginning of 1985 to play a co-ordinating role, particularly in food shipments to the countries of the Sahel. This was a move encouraged by the United States, but much resented by the French who regarded francophone West Africa as their area of influence. WFP officials in the field had to battle against sometimes obstructive African Governments – the Nigerians showed particular disregard for the suffering of fellow Africans – to get relief food through, and WFP knew much more than other agencies about who was doing what. Information was the key to effective co-ordination. Having seen the European Commission's filing system in Brussels, I am quite prepared to believe what I was told in Rome – that WFP had received telephone calls from harassed officials in Brussels asking what the EEC had contributed in food aid to a particular African country.

The establishment of new UN offices in response to the famine did nothing to reduce the brawling between agencies. If anything, it increased it. In an era of static, even declining UN budgets, there were now more agencies competing for limited funds. For UN watchers, there was a fine illustration of the point in June 1985, once again involving Edouard Saouma of the FAO. At issue was a grant of $70,000 from the Dutch Government to buy seeds for Chad. The funds were made available to the FAO, but were diverted by Bradford Morse's Office for Emergency Operations in Africa which proceeded to purchase the seeds. The diversion merited a stiff telegram from Saouma to Morse complaining about the OEOA's assumption of an 'operational' role. 'This was not my understanding of what OEOA was supposed to do,' protested Saouma, 'and I trust that this is not in fact what is intended for the future.' Life in the UN family can be awkward when big brothers fall out.

11

A Weapon of War

On 19 January 1985, some two months after his appointment, Kurt Jansson, the United Nations chief in Addis Ababa, called on Colonel Mengistu, the Ethiopian leader, to present him with some very important proposals. They involved two schemes for bringing relief to huge numbers of people in northern Ethiopia cut off by civil war from any regular food supplies. Mengistu could choose between the two; both involved safe passage for relief convoys.

The first plan had been devised by Jansson himself. He wanted special permission from the Ethiopians for United Nations trucks to travel from Government-occupied territory into rebel-held areas. Convoys should travel north from Makelle, the main town of Tigre region and the furthest north that food now travelled even under military escort, and south from Asmara, capital of Eritrea, to link up on the main road that formed Ethiopia's spinal column. In order to ensure safe passage from the rebel groups, the United Nations would have to make at least informal contact with the two principal guerrilla groups, the Eritrean People's Liberation Front (EPLF) and the Tigrean People's Liberation Front (TPLF). As a token of the importance he attached to the proposal, Jansson told Mengistu that he would lead the first convoy.

The second proposition came from the International Committee of the Red Cross. It reflected the ICRC's greater knowledge of Ethiopian conditions and its greater suspicion of the Ethiopian Government. Like the UN, it wanted to run its own food convoys into guerrilla areas, but it attached a number of conditions. It sought the sensible precaution that Government forces should de-mine roads that they had made impassable for the guerrillas; it insisted that the Red Cross, and not the Ethiopian Relief and Rehabilitation Commission, should distribute all the food as well as organize the convoys; and it demanded that none of the civilians it registered for feeding should be

133

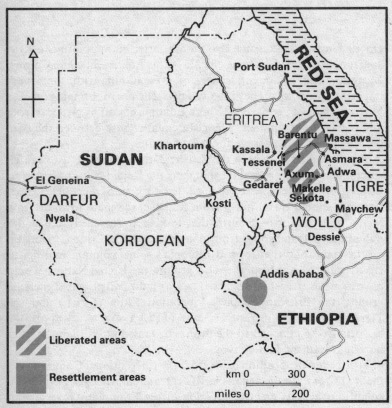

Ethiopia and Sudan: access to liberated areas

liable for the Government's controversial resettlement programme. Just as Jansson had decided to lead the first UN convoy to cross between Government and guerrilla areas, Léon de Riedmatten, head of the ICRC delegation in Ethiopia, reckoned on being in the first Red Cross vehicle. It was a rule that he had long operated: that he would not send any of his drivers where he was not prepared to go himself.

Jansson's discussion with Mengistu in January 1984 marked the culmination of three months of pressure on the Ethiopian authorities to let humanitarian concerns override politics so that food could reach all of those in need. The statistics of people affected were even less reliable on the guerrilla side than in Government territory, but at least three million victims of the famine stood no chance of being reached either by the Government or by agencies working with the Government. They faced the grimmest of all choices as the famine built up to its deadly climax in the autumn of 1984: trek west in the hope of finding food in Sudan; set out for Government feeding centres trusting that they would not be penalised for living in guerrilla areas; or stay at home and face slow death by starvation.

Eritrean and Tigrean civilians were trapped in a vice of famine and civil war. Worse, as the big international aid donors swung into belated action in Ethiopia after the BBC television coverage, there was a danger that they would be simply left out of account. Governments, even Western ones, are loath to deal with the enemies of other Governments, even Marxist ones, and had it not been for private agencies, the tragedy that befell northern Ethiopia towards the end of 1984 would have been on an even vaster scale.

The first outside agency to make a decisive reappraisal of the appalling fate awaiting Eritrean and Tigrean civilians was the radical British charity War on Want. They had had a long association with the relief arms of both liberation fronts, and did nothing to conceal their support for their struggles. In the ideological looking-glass of the Ethiopian conflict, the ruling Marxists in Addis Ababa were pitted against Marxists in the ascendant within both Eritrean and Tigrean freedom movements.

As famine took hold in the two regions, the supply problems on the guerrilla side became overwhelming. Relief agencies operating from Sudan could buy limited quantities of grain on the local market and send it over the border. But crop failure in Sudan was already posing disaster there, and it was no solution to rob one hungry country to feed another. The logistics of bringing foreign grain overland from Port Sudan were equally defiant: it took one month to bring food to central Tigre, most of that time on atrocious roads in guerrilla territory which shook trucks to bits. How much more sensible, reasoned War on Want, if a safe-passage agreement could be secured and food brought direct from one of Ethiopia's own Red Sea ports. Compared with a month from Port Sudan, the journey by laden truck to central Tigre from Massawa was just three days.

War on Want was possibly the Ethiopian Government's least favourite agency, so there was no point in making a direct approach. Instead it gained the backing of fifty-two relief agencies in Europe and Canada, and then approached Willy Brandt, the former West German Chancellor, who agreed to head a commission to monitor safe-passage arrangements. Other political luminaries were then taken on board. They included Pierre Trudeau, former Canadian Prime Minister, Olof Palme, former Swedish Prime Minister, Bruno Kreisky, former Austrian Chancellor, and Joop Van Uyl, a former Dutch premier who was chairman of the Socialist International and particularly anxious to pursue the safe-passage scheme on the ground in Ethiopia. To their impeccable socialist credentials in the developed world, War on Want added the reputation of Léopold Senghor, former President of Senegal. They also approached President Nyerere of Tanzania, then chairman of the Organization for African Unity, but his preparedness to make eloquent appeals on behalf of Africa's starving foundered on the less noble ideal of not wishing to upset the Ethiopian Government.

War on Want's safe-passage scheme progressed rapidly. An implementation committee was set up which began to consider the detail of the operation: how the trucks would be painted; where the emergency landing strips would be located; how the drivers would be recruited, and so on. Both liberation fronts responded positively to the initiative. The EPLF stated that it was ready 'to observe a ceasefire in the areas of conflict where the liberated and Government-controlled zones are joined so that relief agencies can distribute food provided the Dergue [the Ethiopian leadership] agrees to do the same'. The TPLF also accepted the idea and put forward what it called the 'basis for a Safe Passage Agreement'. This stated that an international commission should be formed, that it should operate from a neutral country – both objectives would be realized in the Brandt plan – and that its role would be to 'liaise effectively and openly with the TPLF and the

Dergue'. The safe-passage arrangement would not imply 'any hint that either the Dergue or the TPLF is surrendering present positions held'.

To all these propositions, the Ethiopian Government responded with an obdurate, unyielding and persistent 'No'. It was the cruel expression of a wretched and universal doctrine: that in the contest between humanity and politics, humanity always loses out. The problem for the Ethiopian authorities was the degree of recognition that a safe-passage agreement would imply for the guerrilla groups. Colonel Mengistu himself complained in an interview with Canadian Broadcasting that safe passage might give the liberation groups 'a legal personality and give them a degree of credence. If terrorists are given a degree of prestige, or this kind of prestige, I think this would have very very, dangerous consequences. Not only for Ethiopia, but for the entire world.'

Colonel Mengistu's view received endorsement from some surprising quarters. Mrs Thatcher's Government, for instance, not exactly friendly towards the Ethiopian Marxists, may have spotted the uncomfortable parallel between the 'terrorist' struggles of northern Ethiopia and Northern Ireland, and pronounced in Ethiopia's favour. Prompted by concern about safe passage from the House of Commons Foreign Affairs Committee, the Foreign and Commonwealth Office replied in July 1985: 'While it is disappointing that no such agreement has been reached so far, it is not surprising that the Ethiopian Government should be reluctant to confer recognition upon the rebels by accepting such an agreement and thus condone their activities.' War on Want's proposal for an international commission to see that food got through had been rejected early on by Timothy Raison, Overseas Aid Minister. 'I understand War on Want's anxiety, but believe in present circumstances it is better to use existing mechanisms rather than to think that the response to the crisis is to set up a new body,' he told the Commons in October 1984. Raison did not explain what 'mechanisms' existed to transport food from Government to guerrilla territory because, of course, there were none.

The guerrilla groups were themselves playing politics with people's lives. The very terms of the TPLF's statement about the international commission having to liaise 'effectively and openly' between the two sides suggested that the guerrillas might be as keen to get political advantage from a safe-passage agreement as to get food for their people. In similar fashion, the Eritrean guerrillas declared that the details of any safe-passage agreement should be worked out 'by the parties concerned', and officials of the Eritrean Relief Association acknowledged the implications for their struggle. 'As soon as Ethiopia accepts safe passage,' a senior Eritrean relief official told me in Sudan, 'they are admitting there is a popular movement, and that large areas of their territory are not under their control.'

The Eritreans themselves double-faulted on the safe-passage question later in 1985. As a result of obscure differences between the Eritrean and Tigrean liberation fronts, the EPLF declared their supposed Tigrean allies to be a security risk, and denied them access to the direct route for food supplies from the Sudanese border to central Tigre. The result was that the Relief Society of Tigre, humanitarian arm of the guerrilla group, had to carry food by a longer, slower and more dangerous route. 'The Eritreans have shown exactly the same attitude towards this problem as the Dergue,' commented an official of the International Committee of the Red Cross. 'There is no difference at all.'

All the high-powered efforts to persuade the Ethiopian Government to accept a safe-passage arrangement came to nothing. For public consumption, officials maintained the fiction that it controlled all Ethiopian territory when by most estimates 85 per cent of the countryside of Eritrea and Tigre was either no man's land or under guerrilla control. In private, the issue of conferring a status on the guerrilla groups was always stressed. 'Even if it is done informally through the United Nations,' Kurt Jansson was told by Mengistu at his meeting in January 1985, 'the arrangement implies some sort of agreement between the rebels and the Government which we will not accept.'

Tackled on safe passage at a conference for the African emergency in Geneva in March 1985, Colonel Goshu Wolde, Ethiopia's Foreign Minister, declared: 'There is no precedent in history for such a thing, and the motives for suggesting it are not humanitarian, but political.' The historical precedents may not have been direct parallels, but they certainly existed. Safe-passage agreements were implemented on a number of occasions during Lebanon's chaotic civil war, and at the time of the Nigerian civil war the Red Cross organized a night-time airlift of relief supplies to Biafra. General Yakubu Gowon, the Nigerian Federal leader, protested that this was 'against all conventions'. One day, perhaps, humanity will be the convention.

138

War on Want's safe-passage scheme, always the most promising, ran into what James Firebrace, the agency's programme officer for the Horn of Africa, called a 'total brick wall' from the Ethiopian authorities. 'If we had been able to get a safe-passage agreement, hundreds of thousands of people would not have died,' he said. An historian of the Ethiopian revolution* described the battle plans of an earlier conflict in the Horn – that between Somalia and Ethiopia over the Ogaden – as drawn up 'on the map of hunger', and so it was in the guerrilla struggles of northern Ethiopia. 'Famine proved to be yet another weapon in the arsenal of war,' Firebrace said.

The Ethiopian official who spoke out the most contemptuously of the safe-passage proposals was Berhanu Bayih, a member of the Politburo and Minister of Labour and Social Welfare, who after the revolutionary celebrations in September 1984 was given overall responsibility for the administration's response to the famine. It was he who met Edward Kennedy during the Senator's visit to Ethiopia over Christmas 1984. Kennedy put to him his own proposal for a 'mercy corridor', and Berhanu Bayih replied with the single dismissive utterance, 'Unimaginable!'

When Kurt Jansson had come to the end of the audience with Colonel Mengistu at which the Ethiopian leader had rejected in quite temperate terms the safe-passage proposals of both the UN and the International Committee of the Red Cross, Berhanu Bayih drew him aside. The ICRC plan, involving an operation quite independent of the Ethiopian authorities, was objectionable, Berhanu Bayih said. 'We don't trust the ICRC. They've got the CIA [United States Central Intelligence Agency] with them. The ICRC are one and the same as the CIA.' It was an extraordinary comment on an agency that simply took its political neutrality more seriously than any other at work in Ethiopia during the famine.

The International Committee of the Red Cross had played its first decisive role in Ethiopia at the time of the Italian invasion in 1935. In his book *Warrior Without Weapons*, Dr Marcel Junod, an ICRC delegate to the Government of Emperor Haile Selassie, described a conflict in which, for the first time, civilian targets were deliberately selected for mass bombing raids. In the most infamous of those attacks, the Italian Air Force struck at Dessie, capital of the now

---

* René Lefort, *Ethiopia: An Heretical Revolution*, Zed Press, 1983.

famine-hit region of Wollo. 'Today it is easy to understand the anguish we felt then at the thought that perhaps our own towns and villages would one day suffer the same fate,' wrote Junod. 'After Dessie, Guernica was to follow. Then a little later Warsaw, and in quick succession Rotterdam, London, Coventry, then Aix-la-Chapelle and Berlin – and finally Hiroshima.'

It was another war that brought the ICRC back to Ethiopia. After the Ogaden conflict between Ethiopia and Somalia in 1977–8, the International Red Cross ran a programme to help amputees. By the time the famine struck in areas of northern Ethiopia overtaken by civil war, the ICRC had a unique status among the charitable organizations at work in the country. Not only was Ethiopia a signatory to the Geneva Conventions, but on Christmas Eve 1981 the Government had signed a special 'Status Agreement' with the ICRC which gave it a legal position in Ethiopia denied to other agencies. It meant, in essence, that without the abrogation of an international agreement, the ICRC could not be thrown out. As matters developed in the North, it was probably only that 'Status Agreement' that kept the ICRC at work.

At issue was the Government's treatment of its own people. It was, after all, television images of starvation in the relief camps of Wollo and Tigre that had prompted private generosity and a public response from the West. How much of a priority did the Ethiopian Government now attach to the feeding of these people? We have already seen how an inflated regard for national sovereignty led to the Ethiopian rejection of proposals that people living on the wrong side of the civil war should be fed at all. But the allegations now being made – most vehemently by the ICRC – were even more serious: that the Ethiopian authorities were deliberately withholding food aid from the North because of the political unreliability of the northerners, and that aid was being diverted to already privileged groups like the army and the militia and to the dubious resettlement programme. 'The last priority is given to the North,' an ICRC official said. 'They claim for them, but they don't want to feed them.'

It is a heartbreaking business trying and failing to feed the starving, and in Tigre the hearts of Red Cross workers came very close to breaking. The ICRC calculated in the middle of 1985 that they were feeding around one-quarter of famine victims, and that their operation had reached its ceiling. Indeed, so convinced were they of

Government malevolence towards the Tigreans that they believed that any increase in their programme would merely provide the authorities with an excuse to cut down further on Government feeding. Specific examples were produced of official discrimination against civilians who had reached Government feeding centres from guerrilla-held or 'grey' areas. In the towns of Axum and Adwa, the ICRC said that Ethiopian Red Cross field workers had been threatened with death 'because they were feeding the wrong people', and in Adwa it was claimed that the Ethiopian Relief and Rehabilitation Commission had tried to prevent the Red Cross from providing seeds to farmers who came from areas outside Government control.

The ICRC did not shrink on occasion from making their complaints public. Unlike some other non-official agencies, which were more circumspect in their criticisms, the International Red Cross was unlikely to be expelled for its observations. At a meeting with donors in February 1985, Jean Pierre Hocké, the ICRC's operations director, said: 'Either you just want to send a lot of food to the country, or you really want to help the starving. In the second case, what is happening is unacceptable.'

In trying to sort out who or what was behind the failure of the Ethiopian authorities to bring enough food to the North, the problem is compounded by the inadequacies of their own procedures. The Relief and Rehabilitation Commission has no formal system for accounting to donors on how they have utilized food aid sent to the country. Similarly, no information is available on how the RRC selects priorities in its relief programmes. What is almost certain is that the final say does not rest with the RRC at all, but with higher political authorities, probably the Politburo itself. In a country faced with regular shortages, food becomes a strategic commodity, and in the view of the leadership is likely to be far too important to be left to a bunch of woolly philanthropists, whether Ethiopian or foreign. A parallel might be the fate of energy stocks at the time of a national coal strike in an industrialized economy.

I hesitate to differ from the ICRC in the conclusion they have reached on the basis of eye-witness observations in Tigre, but I believe that there is no proof that the Ethiopian authorities set out deliberately to starve the North. Figures triumphantly produced by journalists in the course of 1985 undoubtedly demonstrated that areas in the North were continuing to go very short of food. It is equally apparent that the régime continued to keep the cities properly fed. But when I revisited Ethiopia in June 1985, there was as much concern about food failing to reach pockets of severe hunger in the South as the North. The truth is that Ethiopian relief officials were being required to juggle between vast and competing needs which could never be met by their meagre transport resources. Much of the blame lay with a system that had consistently discriminated against the rural peasant, whether he was starving or not, but the big Western donors cannot escape their share of responsibility. Ethiopia, both directly and through the United Nations, had been appealing for years for help with transport. Like the food, the trucks started arriving in greater quantity in 1985, and like the food there were too few of them and they were too late.

In Wollo, where Save the Children Fund worked, it was reckoned that 9,000 tonnes of grain were being distributed each month against an estimated requirement of 35,000 tonnes. It meant that many people were going hungry and many people were getting no food at all. But was it deliberate neglect by the Ethiopian authorities? Though still hungry, Wollo was receiving almost what the United Nations in 1984 had allocated for the whole country. Ethiopia's Relief and Rehabilitation Commission was now receiving some 24,000 tonnes of grain a month, so Wollo was getting about a third of relief supplies available to the Government. Part of the problem lay in continuing United States reluctance to supply the RRC with grain, the result of which was that American charities working further north in Eritrea were receiving a disproportionate portion of the share available for the famine zones. Save the Children officials stopped short of blaming the Government. 'Food is definitely not getting to northern Wollo,' David Alexander, the SCF field director told me. 'It could have something to do with trucks being diverted to the resettlement programme, but I don't want to come to the conclusion that they're deliberately starving Korem.'

The argument over feeding the North was nothing compared to the passions roused by the Government's resettlement programme. In the course of 1985 it divided the international aid community down the middle. Western Governments could not agree on the merits of the programme; the private aid agencies held widely different views; and there was no uniform outlook at the United Nations. Some UN agencies became deeply involved in helping the programme; others remained extremely wary of it. For those who sympathized with the scheme, the settlers were 'environmental refugees'; for those who disapproved, they were 'internal deportees'.

The movement of people from the over-populated highlands is as old as Ethiopia itself. With the establishment of the country's modern boundaries in the nineteenth century, it became a more conscious political process and is still resented by those – like the American Indians and the Australian aborigines – whose so-called 'virgin lands' were settled by outsiders. In modern Ethiopia, resettlement from the drought-prone North has long been a feature of Government policy, both Imperial and Revolutionary. With the apparently intensifying famine conditions of the 1970s and 1980s there is no doubt that resettlement is a perfectly valid option for a Government confronted in the North with environmental degradation and human suffering on a vast scale. With international aid-givers unprepared to provide either the funds or the expertise to make the highlands bloom again, mass resettlement is one of the very few options left to the Ethiopian authorities.

What seems to have prompted the huge new impetus given to the resettlement programme at the end of 1984 was the hope of international assistance in the aftermath of famine. As it turned out, the only aid on which the Ethiopians could rely was from the Soviet Union, in particular the twelve Antonov cargo planes, the twenty-four helicopters and the 500 men of the Soviet Air Force flying under the flag of the Soviet civil airline Aeroflot. The target, both by road from Wollo and by air from beleaguered Tigre, was to move 1.5 million people. By the middle of 1985, a third of this number had already been resettled.

The journey from the Ethiopian highlands to the lowland resettlement areas of the South West was long and nasty. The Russians provided more than 300 trucks which were added to an assortment of Ethiopian buses for a road journey of around 1,000 miles. Many of the settlers were already in a wretched state of health, and some died on the way. Most of them were quite unaccustomed to travelling in any form of vehicle, let alone an aircraft. Settlers from Tigre were crammed without any form of seating into the unpressurized cargo holds of the Antonovs for the shuttle from Makelle to Addis Ababa. Many were very ill on the flight and, again, some died.

But the controversy surrounding the resettlement programme was unconnected with conditions on the journey. The issue was whether the selection of migrants was voluntary. Ethiopian relief officials insisted that it was; the International Red Cross working with the starving in the towns of Tigre said it was not. ICRC officials said that settlers selected from famine victims in Axum, mostly able-bodied men, were kept under armed guard in a special compound described as a 'transit camp' in the town. They were given a little food twice a day and were allowed out of the compound only to defecate, and even then under guard. 'This is not voluntary,' a senior ICRC official told me. 'This is deportation. It's like the concentration camps in World War II.'

Eye-witness accounts testifying to the involuntary nature of the programme in other Tigrean towns formed the basis of sharp protests from the ICRC to the Ethiopian Government. Unlike the other private agencies working in Ethiopia, the special status of the ICRC meant that its official dealings were not with Ethiopia's relief commission, but with the Foreign Ministry. By all accounts, there were some towering confrontations between Ministry officials and Léon de Riedmatten, head of the ICRC delegation. On one occasion he was warned to be careful about making accusations of Ethiopian misconduct in the resettlement programme. 'I will not be careful,' replied de Riedmatten. 'I do not want to be a participant in these terrible acts.' On another occasion, the Foreign Ministry complained to de Riedmatten about one of his officials in the field who had been particularly critical of the Ethiopian authorities. 'Mr de Riedmatten, you have a very bad delegate in Maychew,' said the man from the Foreign Ministry. 'It would be better if you remove him.' Léon de Riedmatten responded with a contemptuous 'Never!'

Confirmation that at least part of the resettlement programme was less voluntary than the Government made out came from some of the settlers themselves. Early in 1985, another small refugee exodus began to add to the myriad refugee problems that disfigure the continent of Africa. These were settlers who had been brought from northern Ethiopia, and had then kept on moving. Several thousand of them crossed into Sudan in an effort to return to their homes the long way round. They all claimed to have been resettled against their will, and many had been separated from their families. One was quoted as saying: 'If I can go home and spend one night with my family, I'll go, and if they kill me after that it doesn't matter because life here is useless for me.'

From an administrative point of view, the mass resettlement of 1984-5 could certainly have been better handled. Kurt Jansson, the United Nations chief in Addis Ababa, was critical. 'Resettlement has been far too hasty, and there has not been enough investment to support them,' he told me. 'It would usually take between five to seven years to get a programme of this size going and an investment of around $5,000 per family. It was certainly very silly to say that these settlers would be able to have a harvest and support themselves within a year.' The same point was made by Dr Keith Griffin, President of Magdalen College, Oxford, and a development economist who has studied Ethiopia in detail. He argued that the assistance being provided for the settlers was little more than they were receiving as relief in the North. 'It is most unlikely that Ethiopia has the resources to undertake a resettlement programme of the size envisaged,' Dr Griffin said. 'Indeed, the Government seems to have realized this, but instead of abandoning the programme it has abandoned the settlers.'

If a lack of resources crippled the programme in 1985, there was no question of the political impetus behind it diminishing. In the summer of 1985, Ethiopia's revolutionary leadership ordered the closure of high schools and universities, in most cases before annual examinations had been held, and told students that they would be taken to the West to help the settlers establish their new homes and farms. Convoys of buses that had latterly been full of settlers were now transporting students; Aeroflot was similarly on hand to fly students from more distant corners of the country. Several I spoke to professed themselves quite cheerful at the prospect of this new 'zematcha' or 'military campaign', as these regular revolutionary excursions are known in Ethiopia; an altogether less committed student was presumptuous enough to ask at a public meeting how far his resettlement camp was from the Sudanese border.

Whatever the view of outsiders, the resettlement programme was here to stay. This posed a fresh dilemma for foreign relief workers. Should the settlers – a majority of them certainly volunteers, a minority equally certainly the victims of coercion – now be left to their fate because delicate consciences in the West disapproved of Government methods? As usual, many Western politicians failed to note any moral issue here at all; as usual, it was the private agencies that led the way.

'Somehow, we have to keep struggling to separate humanitarian

145

care from politics,' observed Ralph Wright, a forceful American Red Cross worker who was transferred to the Ethiopian society to help out in the crisis during 1985. As we have seen from the role of the International Committee of the Red Cross, there was unlikely to be uniformity of view on the resettlement question even within the Red Cross community, and Wright had to be cautious in expressing too emphatic a view. But I saw a letter that he wrote to his son Robert in the United States after touring resettlement sites. He identified the desperate needs in medicine, food and trained personnel at a hospital serving newly arrived settlers and wrote: 'This is an emergency, children and adults are dying due to lack of proper nutrition and medical assistance. A plan will be worked out, but it has to be carefully developed because donor societies and donor Governments (the US a prime one) have instructed us that their supplies are not to be used in the resettlement areas.'

The American agency Catholic Relief Services reached a similar conclusion after Father Thomas Fitzpatrick, its field director, visited resettlement areas in January 1985. He described the approach of the voluntary agencies as 'not to do anything to encourage or assist in the actual resettlement; but once the people were resettled and needed assistance, then to respond with humanitarian assistance when requested'. Father Thomas emphasized the need to keep families from the famine areas together; where families had been separated 'they must be united'. Since there was very little prospect of agricultural self-sufficiency in the northern famine zone, the development imperative behind the programme was plain enough, he argued. 'By assisting in the settlement area, there is a good chance that the majority of the settlers will become self-sufficient,' Father Thomas said.

These clearly expressed views by American relief workers had no impact on the outlook of the US Administration towards resettlement. US officials were quoted at the end of 1984 as stating that the programme was little more than an attempt 'to disperse the guerrillas and the population which supports them', and Peter McPherson, administrator of USAID, told a press conference in December 1984 that resettlement should be stopped and 'the money and resources should be used to help the millions facing starvation'. The programme was not stopped, although it may have been slowed because of opposition from major Western donors.

Where the Americans led, their close allies followed. Both Britain and West Germany were hostile to the programme. Whatever else dictated the response of Western nations to the many-sided Ethiopian tragedy, it was not simple humanity. The views of other donor Governments reflected the range of political attitudes towards Ethiopia. Italy, Sweden and Finland accepted the need for a resettlement programme, but would not help. Australia, Canada and Norway supported the programme. The United States imposed an embargo on American grain going to the settlement camps, and so the Ethiopians had to look elsewhere. Canada agreed to supply some, and the World Food Programme of the United Nations received a request for a massive 300,000 tonnes of food for resettlement. Their capacity to supply even a proportion of the request depended as always on the attitude of Governments that held the surpluses.

In the first months of the crash resettlement programme, the European Community maintained an embargo on grain supplies in deference to its more conservative members, but that attitude changed in 1985 to allow small quantities to reach the settlements. Commission officials argued that supplying grain would enable Europe to exercise a certain leverage on the Ethiopian authorities to conduct the programme humanely, and would provide a counter-influence to any Soviet-inspired plans to collectivize agriculture on the settlements. It was an example of the use of aid to gain humanitarian and even strategic advantage – a tactic not favoured by cold warriors in Washington and London.

The British political establishment washed its hands entirely of the resettlement programme, failing even to acknowledge that there might be people who now needed their share of help from the international community. The House of Commons Foreign Affairs Committee, which included some notable Labour Party campaigners like Ian Mikardo and Dennis Canavan, stated simply in its 'Famine in Africa' report: 'Support should not be given to the Ethiopian Government's resettlement schemes unless and until there is clear evidence that it is a properly humanitarian, and not a purely politically motivated scheme.' This was fine by the British Government, which had no intention of helping anyway. 'The first priority must continue to be to feed those still at risk in areas of severe famine,' the Foreign Office told the committee. In keeping with this outlook, British officials did remarkably little during 1985 to appraise the programme for themselves. Whether it was a Marxist plot or a desperate development measure, the British preferred not to know.

At the United Nations, there were pronounced differences of opinion. The General Assembly had actually adopted a resolution calling upon the Secretary-General to mobilize resources for Ethiopia 'including assistance for the victims of drought who wish to resettle in areas less prone to drought'. UNICEF, the United Nations Children's Fund, led the way in bringing assistance to the settlers. It sent supplementary food to children in the settlements and ordered twenty-two milling machines to convert relief grain into flour. With that assistance, they also brought a positive diplomatic influence to bear on the Ethiopian Government by suggesting a three-month hiatus in the resettlement programme. It was the sort of influence which was forfeited by Governments that professed humanitarian motives, but refused to help.

The United Nations Development Programme took a much more wary view of resettlement, despite cogent arguments favouring it from Dr Kenneth King, UNDP's Resident Representative in Addis Ababa. Dr King contended that Ethiopia was now facing a potential double disaster. The area that the settlers had left was unproductive, and without effective aid the new settlement areas would remain so. There was a proposal for a $1.5 million pilot development scheme to benefit settlers from Wollo, but this did not find favour with UNDP headquarters in New York. Bradford Morse, head of the programme and a former US Congressman, told Dr King: 'The United Nations would be supporting the denial of human rights in Ethiopia by supporting resettlement.' Even small grants which in normal circumstances could be made by UNDP's local office were discouraged when headquarters was told that they were intended for resettlement.

It was alleged that the United States was applying pressure on United Nations agencies to turn their backs on the settlements. UNDP is regarded as being particularly vulnerable because the agency is dependent on an annual pledging conference for funds. Bradford Morse reacted indignantly to the suggestion that he had responded to any such pressure. 'My governing council has forty-eight members and I take my orders from them and not from the United States government,' he said.

Some resettlement from the Ethiopian highlands was greeted in the Western world with tremendous acclaim. In 'Operation Moses' more than 7,000 Ethiopian Jews – the Falashas – were evacuated by the Israelis from refugee camps in Sudan between November 1984 and January 1985, when publicity stopped the exercise. This was hailed as the 'Rescue of the Lost Tribe', and the Israelis were credited with another brilliant daredevil operation. It was a rescue that did not always end happily in the Promised Land. There were doubts about the Jewishness of the Falashas, specifically that some may have married outside their faith, and the Chief Rabbi declared that they had to undergo ritual conversion. In the *Observer* newspaper in July 1985, one Ethiopian, Yitzhak Aron, was quoted in nostalgic terms about his home country: 'Everything was fine there; I lived in Addis Ababa with my wife, we both had good jobs and we were not short of money and food.' The Falashas marched in protest against the Chief Rabbi's ruling, and the same report quoted a demonstrator as saying: 'Maybe it would have been better if we had stayed in Ethiopia despite everything we suffered there. At least there we knew who we were. We can put up with most things, but not a blow to our faith.'

In reality, many of the public perceptions formed about Ethiopia in the aftermath of the famine emergency owed more to Western prejudices than to what was happening on the ground. Double standards tended to dictate official attitudes, particularly in the United States where endemic corruption was tolerated in Sudan and relatively minor irregularities pounced upon and magnified in Ethiopia. The Ethiopians never received the benefit of the doubt. Shortages in the North were assumed to be the result of Government policy without proper appraisal of shortages elsewhere in the country, including in the settlement areas. A degree of coercion in resettlement led to major Western donors not only turning their backs on the programme, in itself a legitimate political tactic, but on hundreds of thousands of settlers. It was as if one of the central lessons of the famine had not been absorbed by the official aid-givers: that a generous Western public wanted politics for once to be ignored so that people could be fed.

12

Towards the Sunset

> They trekked for weeks
> They trekked under the sun
> They trekked in darkness ...
> Walking towards sunset ...
> Leaving the land of sunrise
> Overwhelmed by disease
> Tortured by dusty wind ...
> No food to eat
> No water to drink
> No mountain to see
> No trees to cool the heat ...

The poem was written, in English, by a Tigrean. Around 350,000 refugees, both Eritrean and Tigrean, spilled out of northern Ethiopia on the hunger trail to Sudan. With little or no let-up in the war, refugee columns became easy targets for the Ethiopian Air Force. There was also the physical and spiritual hardship of descending from the highlands of home to the hot and featureless deserts of Sudan. But all this was preferable to the greater uncertainties of seeking help from Government feeding centres.

The build-up to disaster in the liberated areas had been well documented by private agencies working with the relief arms of the guerrilla movements. 'The drought in Tigre is getting worse,' declared an Oxfam report in the middle of 1984. 'An estimated 1.4 million people are now seriously affected and living in emergency conditions. This is nearly half a million more than last year.' Tigrean officials stated that some 8,000 people had already died of starvation in the six months up to March 1984. The response from the international community to appeals for help had been meagre. The Relief Society of Tigre (REST) could 'only feed six to seven per cent of the half million people in the west of the region at any one time. Many more are too weak to make the long journey from the drought area,' said Oxfam.

150

'The situation will undoubtedly deteriorate.'

Deteriorate it did. In March 1985 Oxfam produced another report entitled 'Tigre, People in a Multi-Disaster'. The title told its own story. Like the earlier report, it was prepared by Oxfam workers who had themselves to make arduous cross-country journeys, often travelling at night to avoid detection by Ethiopia's air force. 'Famine conditions are widespread and there is a complicated pattern of migration occurring at present,' said the report. 'Those who cannot move are the aged, the handicapped and the sick. They occupy many villages which are otherwise abandoned. These people in particular face a certain death in the very near future if no help is forthcoming.'

After the explosion of international interest in northern Ethiopia in October and November 1984, the focus began to shift to the refugee fall-out in Sudan. On just one day in December, 16,000 refugees crossed the border heading for camps near the Sudanese towns of Kassala and Gedaref. There had been refugees here since the 1960s, but camps which a few months before had been looking after a few thousand were now having to accommodate a tenfold increase. Slow though it was to materialize, Western aid donors provided substantial assistance for the refugees in Sudan. But a better, certainly a longer-term answer lay in providing effective help within guerrilla-controlled territory. It was also the only answer for those too weak to move.

Here was a challenge for an international aid community that kept saying it put people first. Were civilians who happened to live on the wrong, that is to say anti-Government, side in a civil war to receive proper assistance? How much would they get and how would it be delivered? No one who has read this far will be surprised to learn that the answer to these questions, provided by the big aid agencies of the 1980s, involved the customary trade-off between politics and humanity.

Some players in the international aid game fell back exclusively on their own voluntary agencies. The British Overseas Development Administration, for instance, committed emergency aid from Miss Cherry's Disaster Unit through a body called the Emergency Relief Desk in Khartoum, the Sudanese capital. This was a group of Protestant aid agencies linked to the Eritrean and Tigrean relief organizations. 'The British have worked through non-governmental organizations,' said James Firebrace, of War on Want. 'The extent may be derisory, but at least they have helped.' What the guerrilla-held areas needed, of course, was large quantities of food and the means to transport it. For that, they had to look to those with greater capacity: the United States and the European Community.

The politics of the region indicated a favourable response from Washington. The Administration was at daggers drawn with the Ethiopian Government, and though themselves Marxists, the guerrillas had the merit of opposing the Soviet Union's principal client in the Horn of Africa. Sudan's sandy vastness was regarded by the Americans, somewhat improbably, as a rampart against the expansion of Soviet influence, and Administration officials made a regular point of complimenting their ally on the generosity displayed towards other countries' refugees. As well as the great influx of Tigreans and Eritreans, there were also some 250,000 Ugandans, 121,000 Chadians and 5,000 Zaireans seeking refuge in Sudan at the beginning of 1985. How natural that the United States should contemplate action to stem the flow of further migration from Ethiopia by providing timely cross-border aid.

The need was clearly identified by American aid officials as the human haemorrhage across the border into Sudan intensified at the turn of the year. Peter McPherson, head of the United States Agency for International Development (USAID), told a House of Representatives hearing in February: 'The problem which bothers me the most right now is northern Ethiopia where there are two to three million people, where we are simply not able to get enough food into that area.' A policy response to the problem began to emerge and, at the beginning of March, McPherson was able to be more forthright about helping people threatened with starvation. He wrote in the *Washington Post* that the United States was 'determined to do whatever we can to avoid it. We believe the international community cannot turn from the problem. If that means being charged with "political" motives for humanitarian action, so be it. We must do everything in our power to see the hungry fed.'

McPherson's robust comments about doing 'everything in our power' came at the start of a tour of famine-hit countries by Vice-President George Bush. During his stay in Sudan, Bush toured refugee camps near the Ethiopian border, and while not exactly shaking his fist at the Communists in Addis Ababa, made it plain how American official thinking was developing. He appealed to Colonel Mengistu to 'give a little' and resurrected the notion of safe passage for food convoys within Ethiopia: 'The situation cries out for safe passage and safe delivery of food for Eritrea and Tigre, and let politics be put aside.'

Senior USAID officials were meanwhile in discussion in Khartoum with representatives of the relief wings of the two guerrilla movements. There were also talks, both in Sudan and in the United States, with outside agencies which might become the instruments of a mightily stepped-up cross-border relief operation. This was 'can-do' America in action with talk of mobile workshops, teams of mechanics and 300 trucks being shipped in to play 'cat-and-mouse' with the MiGs of the Ethiopian Air Force on the mountain passes of Eritrea and Tigre. The intended scale of the US operation can best be judged by the fact that in December 1984 the Eritrean Relief Association had just nine trucks. It managed to borrow more from the fighters, but could bring in only enough food to keep 140,000 people fed, about a tenth of the people in need. Tigrean relief workers confronted by longer and more arduous journeys had access to forty-five lorries delivering grain on a regular basis to about 70,000 people.

The International Committee of the Red Cross was approached by the Americans and asked if they would be interested in taking delivery of 210 trucks. Wisely, Red Cross officials decided to wait and see, and were unsurprised when after several months none of the trucks on offer had been sighted. 'This US operation has been like the wind in Khartoum,' said an ICRC official. 'One day it's in the West; the next day it's in the South – on and off like that.' Another agency involved was a tiny American organization, Mercy Corps International, which had had a modest seed and grain distribution scheme in Tigre. When I visited their freshly painted Khartoum office in July 1985, four months after the Bush visit, I was told they were still waiting for twenty-six trucks. In the meantime, Mercy Corps seemed to have frustratingly little to do.

After his tour of refugee camps in Sudan, Vice-President Bush travelled on to Geneva to attend a big United Nations fund-raising conference for Africa. It may have been the Swiss mountain air or the two hours the Vice-President spent with Ethiopia's Foreign Minister, Colonel Goshu Wolde, but he seemed to undergo a change of heart about the cross-border operation, and with it American foreign policy shifted as well. In one of those occasional bureaucratic slips that enable outsiders to observe policy changes at work, Bush did not deliver the advance text of his speech to the UN conference. What he said was a significantly toned-down version of his original strictures on Ethiopian and international failure to get food to people on the guerrilla side.

'Nearly eight million people are affected [in Ethiopia] and many of them are beyond the reach of any existing feeding programmes,' the Vice-President said. 'That simply cannot continue. We respect the sovereignty and territorial integrity of Ethiopia. That is not the issue.' In the original version Bush then called for a truce between the Government in Addis Ababa and 'its armed opponents' to allow food to proceed to 'all in need'. In the speech as delivered, Bush said: 'All concerned – all – must put aside politics to bring relief to all in need.' The implication of this change was that the United States had rather lost interest in the idea of safe passage. The next change was the deletion of a reference to 'a conspiracy of silence' about 2.5 million people starving in guerrilla-held areas. In the Geneva conference hall, Bush spoke only of the United States not accepting silence.

Washington was developing a classic 'carrot and stick' squeeze on the Marxists in Addis Ababa. American food aid had begun to flow in large quantities into Government areas, and this meant a steadily expanding role for trusted American voluntary agencies in the field. Here was a 'carrot' for the Ethiopians and more influence for the United States. The 'stick' was represented by the threat to start up a big cross-border operation with all that that implied for US relations with the guerrillas. The whole point about a 'carrot and stick' exercise is that the stick is either sparingly used, or never used at all. Somewhere in this cleverly crafted foreign policy structure, the interests of a lot of hungry civilians were being sacrificed.

Fresh military developments in the civil war could have influenced United States policy-makers. As Vice-President Bush toured the refugee camps of eastern Sudan and travelled on to Switzerland, the Ethiopian army was opening up its Eighth Offensive against Tigrean guerrillas. Although the Ethiopians never talked about it, and the Tigreans never admitted it, the fact is that in nine weeks of fighting the guerrillas received a very bloody nose. One knowledgeable foreign relief worker told me that the Government offensive had 'completely uprooted' both the fighters of the TPLF and the aid workers of REST in their principal strongholds in central and western Tigre.

The guerrillas conceded that their relief efforts in Tigre had been disrupted and that refugee routes to and from Sudan had been attacked. 'The Dergue was temporarily successful in its aim,' said the TPLF at the end of the offensive. 'People were displaced from their villages, much of what they owned was stolen or destroyed and the relief operation was disrupted ...' The famine itself had been a big factor in the progress of the fighting. It had left Tigrean civilians very weak and thus unable to 'participate as usual'. The TPLF also claimed that the provision of Western food aid had directly helped Government forces. 'This was because there was a steady supply of donated international community food which they helped themselves to,' said the TPLF. 'This, coupled with the airlifts of the United Kingdom, France and Germany, meant that the food was exactly where they needed it at this time. Transport was also made easy for them as they used the trucks ostensibly meant for the distribution of famine relief for their military activities.'

Some have argued that American policy planners banked on the success of this offensive in deciding drastically to scale down their plans for a cross-border relief operation from Sudan. Such an elaborate conspiracy is implausible. In Ethiopia's civil wars, there are no permanent gains, only temporary advantages, and so it proved in the aftermath of the Eighth Offensive as Government forces were harried back into their garrison towns. It was never likely that the offensive in itself would provide Government access to a substantially greater number of famine victims.

Having first raised the hopes of those who struggled to bring food to civilians in guerrilla territory, American machinations had now dashed them. 'They never delivered,' said James Firebrace of War on Want. 'They wanted it to be an "American" operation across the border, yet the level of US support to the operation has been pathetic. Their particular crime is that by promising assistance they discouraged others from helping.'

Nearer to home, War on Want tried to get substantial support from the European Community for feeding programmes in Eritrea and Tigre. They were encouraged by resolutions of the European Parliament favouring an evenly balanced approach to a country torn apart by civil war. Motivated largely by its suspicions of aid mismanagement by the Ethiopian régime, the European Parliament resolved in April 1983 that 'emergency aid may be channelled through suitable non-governmental organizations and suitable international

agencies *operating in all parts of the region affected ...*' (my italics).
Parliament repeated this injunction after the Ethiopian famine
became headline news at the end of 1984, and Edgard Pisani, the
European Aid Commissioner, responded in the course of a
Parliamentary debate with Gallic fulsomeness. 'Our only concern is
the interests of people suffering from hunger,' he said. 'With the help
of non-governmental organizations, we are going to areas which are
not under the control of the Ethiopian Government.' His Italian
successor, Lorenzo Natali, who took over at the beginning of 1985,
issued a similar assurance in answer to a Parliamentary question: 'The
Commission attempts to ensure that all affected regions and
populations of Ethiopia are reached despite the warfare in the
country.'

That was the rhetoric of Europe's outlook; the reality was different.
The European Community is tied by treaty arrangement to Ethiopia
under the Lomé conventions which govern Europe's relations with
developing countries. Whatever the European Parliament may have
resolved and whatever Commission officials may have said in public,
it was not a simple matter to provide formal aid to guerrilla groups in
rebellion against a treaty partner. 'It is frankly difficult for us to use the
European Development Fund to intervene in parts of a country not
controlled by the Government,' I was told by a senior Commission
official in Brussels. There was another problem. The Ethiopians had a
particularly sharp group of diplomats accredited to the European
Commission, and one of their pastimes was spotting and protesting at
shipments of aid to the guerrillas. On one occasion an aid shipment
destined for Port Sudan was posted in the *Official Gazette* in Brussels
as 'To the People of Ethiopia'. Ethiopian diplomats intervened to
point out, quite reasonably, that if the Ethiopian people were to be the
beneficiaries, then the shipment need not go to Sudan.

War on Want chose to believe what was said in public and
consequently found itself particularly frustrated by the European
response. As the famine crisis grew during 1984, emergency funds were
required in a hurry. War on Want asked for £630,000 to pay the
running costs of a fleet of forty trucks, ferrying relief grain over the
border from Sudan. The enterprise was vital if people were to be fed at
home and a larger refugee tragedy averted. But the fine words of the
European Parliament counted for little, and six months later nothing
had happened. 'We rather gave up,' James Firebrace, for War on

Want, told me. 'There comes a time when it's no longer worth hammering at the door. If the EEC had come into the picture at an earlier stage and in a big enough way there wouldn't have been a refugee crisis in Sudan. The EEC could have made a vast difference.' It was the diplomacy of participating in a cross-border relief operation that prevented effective European action. A Dutch voluntary agency also involved in the operation was told by the European Commission office in Addis Ababa: 'We must respect the territorial integrity of the country to which the delegation is accredited.' Over the years in Ethiopia many lives have been sacrificed to uphold the time-worn notion of national sovereignty.

The European Commission made one significant gesture towards the people of Eritrea and Tigre during the famine crisis. It sometimes seemed to private agencies to be a scheme of labyrinthine ingenuity and it did not always work, but at least an effort was being made. 'We have to help Eritrea and Tigre,' a Brussels official told me, 'but it has to be done discreetly.' What the Commission proposed was a 'switch' arrangement whereby a private agency would go ahead with an emergency project in guerrilla territory and be compensated by a matching grant for its programme in Government-held Ethiopian territory or even elsewhere. In this way a humanitarian duty could be discharged and diplomatic trouble with the Ethiopian Government avoided. Even that industrious talking-shop the European Parliament was kept in the dark. 'The less we speak about these arrangements the better it is,' I was told. 'We reply to Parliament without any discourtesy, but we don't give them details.'

One of the private agencies to try and take advantage of 'the switch' was Oxfam. It turned out to be a fairly trying experience. The 'switch' would be between an above-board Oxfam scheme in Sudan, which the Commission could be seen to be supporting, and a programme of supplementary feeding for children which included cross-border operations into Eritrea and Tigre. Oxfam would receive £1.2 million from the EEC. So far, so good. Then the problems began. First, the EEC wanted three tenders for the supplementary foods. 'I was telling this EEC bloke that a lot of this stuff was on its way, and that we still hadn't had all their procedures,' said Tony Vaux, of Oxfam's disasters office. Then Oxfam was informed that all the bags of supplementary food had to be clearly marked 'Gift of the EEC', and that there had to be a plaque saying something similar on the side of the delivery trucks.

Vaux described the demands as 'Kafkaesque'; it was certainly a novel way of keeping the arrangement under wraps.

The basic problem was that of squaring the imperatives of alert voluntary agencies with those of a Continental trading arrangement. In November 1984, Oxfam asked Brussels for 500 tonnes of butter oil to be shipped on the *Link Target* sailing to Ethiopia. By the time Brussels had granted the request, the *Link Target* had not only sailed, but had arrived at the other end. Oxfam said it would still like the butter oil, but could it be used in Tigre? Brussels agreed in March, but sent paperwork to Oxford specifying that the butter oil was destined for southern Ethiopia. The 500 tonnes finally arrived in Port Sudan in August, nine months after the initial request. 'Nobody can rely on that sort of operation, that's our conclusion with the EEC,' said Tony Vaux. 'There surely must be better procedures for emergencies.'

There was another exasperated complaint from the private agencies as the European Commission geared up to the famine: the stupefying amount of paperwork required to account for each European Commission grant. The Christian Relief Development Association, umbrella organization for the relief agencies in Addis Ababa which co-ordinated much of the emergency transport, was caught squarely between two overblown bureaucracies, one Ethiopian and one European. The Commission was prepared to pay internal transport costs on most of its food aid. For the CRDA, a simple cash receipt from the Ethiopian authorities was enough, but the EEC required dispatch papers and receipt papers in addition to haulage receipts. When I visited the CRDA's offices they had just sent four box-files full of receipts round to the EEC office to account for their latest transport grant. At Oxfam, Tony Vaux told me that the receipts required by the EEC were so numerous and so complicated that the agency might end up forfeiting the grant it had been offered by Brussels.

Of all the big aid organizations, the one most likely to be able to help the Eritreans and Tigreans, at least in Sudan, was the specialist agency, the United Nations High Commissioner for Refugees (UNHCR). With more than one million refugees in the country, Sudan already had one of the world's largest UNHCR establishments. There were offices in southern Sudan for Ugandan and Zairean refugees, an office in the far West for the Chadians, and the UNHCR offices in the East were greatly reinforced as new refugees from Ethiopia began flooding across the border at the end of 1984.

UNHCR's humanitarian brief brings it fairly frequently into conflict with Governments which would often prefer their refugees to be disregarded. 'We're used to helping people despite the disinclination of Governments,' a UNHCR official said. 'We're used to walking a narrow line and expect a certain amount of Government criticism.' The refugee exodus into eastern Sudan was no exception. Just as the Ethiopian régime had been accused of using resettlement to depopulate its rebellious northern regions, so Ethiopian officials claimed that the rebels were sending their old people, women and children over the border to keep their fighting hand free. Goshu Wolde, Ethiopia's Foreign Minister, argued that the UNHCR camps in Sudan were an 'incitement to the rebels'. The criticism was calmly deflected by UNHCR.

A more pointed challenge to its humanitarian objectives arose in April 1985 when numbers of Tigrean refugees began returning across the border. This movement, partly spontaneous and partly organized by Tigrean relief workers, caused concern and controversy among foreign aid officials. UNHCR was itself dubious when conditions in the highlands had certainly not improved, and United States officials were for a time flatly opposed. Tigrean relief workers tried to ensure that only heads of family embarked on the long trek back to the highlands to prepare for the rains, but whole families insisted on joining their menfolk, including malnourished children too weak to travel. I suspect it was wrong to discourage the movement back. These people may have been fed in the border camps of Sudan, but they were a long way from their home, both physically and spiritually. In the words of the poem that began this chapter, there was in the Sudanese desert 'No mountain to see, No trees to cool the heat ...'

To minimize the risk to life on their journey home, and when back in their villages, the 55,000 Tigreans who crossed the border between April and June 1985 needed food. They also needed blankets and kitchen utensils to resume life in the highlands, and if there was to be a harvest at the end of 1985 they needed seeds and tools.

From UNHCR, they got very little of this. Some food was unofficially distributed, and a blind eye was apparently turned to the use of some UNHCR trucks to transport refugees back to the border. But that was the limit. Private agencies putting pressure on UNHCR to help at the beginning of the big return in April were told: 'In the absence of any request for a programme from either Ethiopia, Sudan

159

or the General Assembly, we do not feel in a position to take an active role in this particular returnee programme, all the more so because it is directed towards the areas of Ethiopia which are contested.' The diplomacy, not the humanity, of the situation dictated that a returning refugee could only be aided when he was, in the UN's terminology, 're-availing himself of the protection of the authorities in his country of origin', and so the Tigreans who merely wanted to go home could not be helped. I pursued the matter with a senior UNHCR official and was told finally that this was 'an undecided question'. It was an inadequate response; the question had already been decided for 55,000 Tigreans.

Where the world's powerful official institutions might have helped most of all was in the matter of promoting peace in Ethiopia's ruinous civil war. In every other area of humanitarian endeavour, the small unofficial agencies had led the way, but there was an awareness that much of their effort was nullified by the continuing conflict. It was no accident that four of the African countries worst affected by famine in 1984–5 – Ethiopia, Chad, Angola and Mozambique – were torn apart by civil wars, all of them owing much to the imported ideological rivalries of the industrialized world. Around half of the Ethiopian Government's entire budget goes on military expenditure – after South Africa, Ethiopia has the best equipped army in Africa – and a similarly large proportion of local resources goes to support the anti-Government struggle. The cost and the insecurity of warfare are the surest guarantee of continuing poverty and famine. 'What is needed', said an Oxfam publication, 'Lessons to be Learned', 'is an initiative which will see a peaceful resolution of the dispute so that the urgent needs of the local populations can be addressed and long-term projects either introduced or extended.'

There were half-hints during 1985 that the Russians might have been making some tentative moves towards promoting an Ethiopian accommodation. Any success would secure yet more Soviet influence in the region. But no Western Government seemed to give the matter much thought, and the United Nations, which had had peculiar responsibility for the initiation of the Eritrean conflict, remained equally inert. The partial approach to the problem represented by Willy Brandt's safe-passage commission had been instigated by a British charity and had fizzled out anyway. There may have been political and material reaction in the West to Africa's desperate troubles, but very little statesmanship had been shown.

Fighting in Ethiopia's guerrilla conflicts actually intensified in 1985. As we have already noted, the Government conducted a major eight-week offensive against the Tigreans during the spring, recapturing the important town of Sekota from the guerrillas. But further north, Government forces for a time lost ground to the Eritrean guerrillas. At the beginning of 1984, guerrillas captured Tessenei, near the Sudan border, and there were other gains in the months before the worst of the famine imposed a truce of hunger on the two sides. In July 1985, Eritrean fighters captured the town of Barentu, their most important gain in some years. Then, during the autumn, both Barentu and Tessenei fell again to Government forces. None of this filled bellies. 'War and drought,' runs a Somali proverb, 'peace and milk.'

In the confusion of a country at war with itself, international aid-givers were presented with a series of dilemmas and opportunities. They fluffed most of them. The ideal was easy enough to articulate: that relief should be given impartially, on the basis of need. But when it came to the test, very few official institutions managed to live up to the ideal. Their failure was best summed up by Tigrean relief representatives. 'If agencies are to remain truly non-political,' observed the Relief Society of Tigre, 'they must stop making decisions about the rights and wrongs of the Tigrean struggle and attempt to assist *all* people in need in Ethiopia, regardless of which side of the conflict they are on.'

13

Privatizing the Famine

The town of El Geneina is as near as you can get to the middle of Africa. It is way out in western Sudan, just short of the border with Chad. When you arrive there, it is only a few miles further to the Atlantic Ocean than to the Red Sea. El Geneina means 'The Garden', and even in the dry season it can be seen from the air as a dizzying splash of green in the vastness of scrubby desert. In the rains, if the rains come, El Geneina is often marooned as dry wadis become broad rivers and the tracks that act as roads in rural Sudan are submerged by flood waters. In the middle of 1985, the rains were the best for a decade. That was good news for farmers anxious to plant for the next harvest; it was grim news for those dependent on relief.

Western Sudan marks one of the world's frontiers against the encroaching desert. Whole areas that were until quite recently under the plough are now under sand. It is said that the Sahara advances up to ten kilometres a year; the pace is at its quickest during periods of drought. Hundreds of villages in the far west of Sudan were simply abandoned as drought and attendant famine tightened their grip during 1984 and 1985. To this migration was added another: more than 120,000 people crossed the border from Chad, refugees both from the expanding desert and from their country's civil commotion.

Famine in western Sudan did not make for easy press coverage. This was an awkward place to reach, and even from El Geneina it was hours of arduous travel to where people were dying of starvation. Apart from refugee camps for the Chadians, there were few of those major concentrations of the hungry which were often convenient for the media and for aid workers, but for the people themselves represented communities in final collapse. Yet the distress was as widespread and as poignant as anything in Ethiopia. When I was in El Geneina in July 1985, Peter Verney, the Save the Children Fund field officer, received an SOS from the police in a village called Beida near the Chad border. Food was needed urgently, but with fifteen children dying daily they had also run out of material for shrouds, and could SCF please send some? 'Children are being buried without shrouds,' Verney observed. 'A psychological barrier has been crossed.'

Almost twenty years ago I had worked as a voluntary teacher in Sudan and some of the kitchen Arabic I picked up then came back to me in El Geneina. When I visited a nearby Chadian relief camp, a little boy followed me for a time and repeated over and over again '*Akil ma fi*'. It meant 'There is no food' or 'I have no food', and it troubled me more that I could understand the simple force of what he was saying.

For much of 1985, a terrible calamity was being predicted for western Sudan. It was said that half a million people or more could perish. No one knows how many did die, but spokesmen for the big official agencies stated on occasions that this calamity was going to be or already had been averted. It was a comforting judgement. Certainly there were unlikely to be those troubling images of mass starvation and death on camera that prompted the public's searching questions about what the aid agencies had been doing in Ethiopia. But it would be wrong to derive too much reassurance from the inaccessibility of starvation in the Darfur region of Sudan. Near El Geneina, I met Ann Dalrymple Smith, an experienced Oxfam nurse who had spent another exhausting morning conducting a nutrition survey among villagers. I asked her what she thought was going to happen. 'This is not just a disaster around the corner,' she said. 'With 50 per cent malnutrition rates, it is already here.'

In June 1985, Oxfam and UNICEF had completed their first extensive nutrition survey of the region. 'In the centres with large numbers of weak children living in poor conditions, illnesses and malnutrition interact strongly,' the report said. 'Many children have died or will die.' What was remarkable about the Oxfam/UNICEF study was not the now familiar litany of weight-for-height ratios, mid-upper arm circumference measurements and all the other ways in which statistics are applied to what is often obvious to the naked eye, but the way in which these two agencies, one private and one official, found huge fault in the aid operation to date.

'The needs of Darfur and the difficulties in providing them were clearly identified in late 1984,' said the report, 'yet Darfur faces a crisis now.' It referred to the plans of United States aid officials to bring relief food to Darfur: 'It seemed that the disaster which was threatened could be averted. Six months later, Darfur is making the headlines for being a disaster – the promise had not been fulfilled.' The original target had been to distribute 500 grams of food per person per day among famine victims in the rural areas. The report found that on average people were receiving a miserable 14 grams a day. 'The USAID dura [sorghum] was intended for the most needy, and this has always been stressed,' the report continued. 'But in practice it has been spread throughout Darfur, with the weakest often receiving the least.' Instead of being devoted entirely to those worst affected by famine, a third of the available grain had been sold at low cost in the towns. Thus 200,000 townspeople had benefited from a third of the grain, and what was left was distributed among one million hungry people in the countryside.

The report was also critical of the failure to distribute enough seed. 'USAID were due to provide 2,000 tonnes of sorghum and 1,000 tonnes of millet seed for northern Darfur, but much of this has yet to arrive, with the optimum planting period imminent,' it said. This was unfortunate because 'the need for provision of seed in June was clear from last December onwards'. But the crucial breakdown had been in food supplies. 'It is regrettable that still, with the rains imminent, there are virtually no food stocks in the region and expensive, desperate measures are having to be taken,' said the report.

The 'expensive and desperate measures' referred to the much-publicized European Community airlift in Sudan. The West German Luftwaffe, the Belgian Air Force, and an ageing Hercules chartered by the British Government for Save the Children were all pressed into service to fly food to the West. In El Geneina, two and a half hours' flying time from Khartoum, they used an airstrip laid down during World War II for ferrying fighters across Africa to the desert war. The runway had hardly been touched since then, let alone maintained. The economics of this operation made even less sense than those of the airlift in Ethiopia. To fly a Hercules to El Geneina and back cost £10,000, enough to buy a truck and its cargo outright. Put another way, a Hercules required 11 tonnes of aviation fuel to deliver about 12 tonnes of food. Such were the equations calmly contemplated when aid officials had failed to get the food through by more sensible means. 'When you see C130 Hercules flying,' one diplomat was quoted as saying, 'you know someone has badly goofed.'

Sudan was America's baby. The scale of the emerging food crisis was first noted by American aid officials as early as March 1984, and it was they who predicted, quantified and responded to it. The United States never publicly stated that the handling of Sudan's food emergency would present the world with an object-lesson in how the Western superpower looked after its friends, but everything about the American operation pointed to the promotion of a deliberate contrast with the limitations of Soviet assistance to Ethiopia and with the workings of a socialist state struck by famine. Sudan had become the largest recipient of United States aid in sub-Saharan Africa – $1 billion during the Reagan years alone – and its people would not be allowed to starve.

In contrast to the slowness with which the United States responded to the build-up of the famine in Ethiopia, USAID outpaced all other official agencies in its reaction to the Sudan emergency. By July 1984, the USAID office in Khartoum was telling Washington that Sudan's harvest would be 50 per cent below normal; by September, a request for 82,000 tonnes of grain had been formulated, processed and approved; in November, the first of the shipments reached Port Sudan. The greatest challenge in Sudan would always be to bring enough help to the two to three million people at risk in the far west of the country. An American likened the exercise to shipping food to New York and then having to transport it to Minneapolis, Chicago and St Louis when the only two-lane highway ran out at Pittsburgh. It was no ideological accident in the circumstances that United States officials chose a private company for the undertaking.

Arkel-Talab Cargo Services Ltd is a twinning of American and Sudanese capital with its head office in Baton Rouge, Louisiana. Its general manager is B. K. Anderson – known to staff simply as 'BK' – who was transport consultant for Arkel International's construction of a sugar refinery in Sudan in the mid-1970s. Arkel was also involved in Chevron's 1,000-mile pipeline from the southern Sudan to the Red Sea – abandoned when Sudan's civil war started up again – and then joined forces with the Talabs, one of Sudan's leading merchant families. The joint company's American accounting procedures, its major workshops at Port Sudan and internal radio network made Arkel-Talab a natural choice for USAID officials looking for a way to win the West.

In the course of the famine, Arkel-Talab won two huge haulage contracts from USAID. The first was signed in November 1984 for the

165

transport of the 82,000 tonnes. In company parlance, this was 'Project-West Sorghum 1'. The grain was delivered in the course of four months to April 1985, and the contract was generally accounted a success. The company lost only 1 per cent of the grain transported, a tiny proportion by Sudanese standards, and the delays that did occur were the result of ships failing to arrive on schedule in Port Sudan – not the company's responsibility. 'We got a lot of good press on that contract,' said a senior company spokesman. 'So did USAID. Compared with what was happening in Ethiopia at the time, everyone got a good press.'

The second contract was signed in April 1985 for the transport of a further 250,000 tonnes of grain to the West. This was 'Project-West Sorghum 2', and it ran into trouble before the ink was dry. Arkel-Talab's main warehouses for supplying the far West were in the town of Kosti, south of Khartoum on the White Nile and a major railway depot. In April these warehouses were attacked during food riots and more than 2,000 tonnes of grain were looted. This may have benefited some of the hungry Sudanese who had trekked into Kosti from the west, but it was not the orderly distribution that USAID and Arkel-Talab had in mind.

After that setback, the contract was set to run from 5 May and was to be completed in 120 days. There was added urgency because the rains were due in July and they would threaten the already tenuous links with the West. The first 800 miles of the journey from Port Sudan to Kosti were easy enough on a black-top highway. West of Kosti the roads ran out, and Arkel-Talab was planning to rely on the railway line to Nyala that the British had laid down in 1906. This was another 700-mile journey. Even Nyala was not the end of the road. It was then taking as much as two weeks for trucks to deliver food to communities in distress near the Chad frontier.

For the Darfur region to be secure in food for the rains, Arkel-Talab had to deliver 1,800 tonnes of grain a day to the railhead during May, June and July. This was to be the American pioneer spirit in action, but the American pioneers never had to contend with Sudan Railways. When I visited western Sudan in early July, grain deliveries to Nyala were down to 180 tonnes, one-tenth of the intended daily total. Even in Arkel-Talab's offices in Khartoum, they were claiming an average for the contract of no more than 440 tonnes, less than a quarter of what was required.

At Sudan's independence, the railway network was handling some three million tonnes of goods a year; it now manages much less than half that figure. 'What's been happening in the meantime is called development,' a senior United Nations official drily observed. Arkel-Talab were evidently unwise to rely as heavily as they did on the railway system, but even they could not have fully anticipated the forces of inertia and corruption they were pitted against. For much of Ramadan, for instance, railway managers appeared to give greater priority to hauling sugar and other items for the festival period than to getting basic foodstuffs to the West. Wagons that should have been full of grain often travelled empty because they had been 'reserved' by merchants along the way. Worse, thousands of tonnes of grain was despatched from Kosti, but 'disappeared' *en route* for Nyala.

Excellent rains finally put paid to any hopes that Arkel-Talab might have had of getting level with the deliveries needed to keep Darfur properly fed. On numerous occasions during late July and August, sections of the railway line were washed away by flood-waters, and laborious engineering repairs had to be conducted. One of the first of these wash-outs caused a derailment which for a time presented an even bigger obstacle to smooth food deliveries to the West.

Arkel-Talab's failure to deliver was a blow, if not a mortal one, to United States pretensions in the field of famine prevention. 'By believing that they could do enough to establish a proper stockpile for the rainy season out here,' said a Save the Children field officer in western Sudan, 'the Americans failed to do anything by way of contingency planning like building bridges and so on.' Some of this might have had the effect, but did not, of muting official United States criticism of the relief operation in neighbouring Ethiopia. There the Ethiopians, not a foreign power, were in charge, and yet the lessons were the same: emergencies are not easily dealt with in large, impoverished Third World countries.

At the beginning of 1985, the United States made it clear that it would handle the crisis in western Sudan, and that it needed little or no assistance from any other official quarter. Dr Bob Brown, director of USAID in Sudan, was not for nothing known in Khartoum as 'Deputy President of Sudan'. He found himself addressing one of the first meetings of the country's new Transitional Military Council in May 1985 after the overthrow of President Gaafar Numeiry. He outlined the desperate relief and logistics problems in the West, and

167

concluded with a flourish: 'Gentlemen, it is for you to decide what the priorities are to be.' In an interview in July, Dr Brown denied that the US had tried to exclude other major agencies from operating in the West – 'We didn't set out to run the world' – but acknowledged that 'Project West' had not turned out to be an American success story. 'There's no way we'll get out of this in the clear. But remember, this is tough on us as well. It's chewed up my staff here. People get very, very tired.'

The breakdown in food supplies to the West gave the other major aid bureaucracies, the United Nations and the European Community, a chance to revive their own flagging performance in the Sudanese relief operation. Both had been left way behind by the Americans in their early response to the emergency. Arkel-Talab's embarrassment now forced USAID to agree that the company should no longer have exclusive access to American food aid destined for the West. Europe already had its airlift, and now both the Commission and the United Nations proposed independent trucking operations to take food across the desert, avoiding the disastrous railway bottleneck.

Europe's slow response to the Sudanese emergency was linked at the start to President Numeiry's refusal to admit that his country was facing a major famine. Only a few years before Numeiry had been saying that Sudan would be a 'bread basket' for the Middle East, and he was disinclined to make the sort of appeal to the international community that his Marxist antagonists had made in Ethiopia. Since the United States had taken the initiative in arranging major food aid shipments before Sudan had even declared an emergency, Numeiry was apparently confident that his American allies could continue to look after his country's food problems.

This was no comfort to European politicians who wanted to see swift action on the basis of aid allocations made after the Dublin summit in December. There was criticism from a group of British Members of Parliament who toured Sudan in February 1985. They demanded to know why only 7,000 of 42,000 tonnes of European food aid had reached the country. The reason, it emerged, was that there had been three months of futile discussion between European and Sudanese officials over the form in which this aid would be acceptable. The Sudanese, believing perhaps that they already had enough free food from the Americans, wanted to sell it, but the Europeans were emphatic that it should be for free distribution. Shortly after the

Commission was publicly dressed down by the British MPs, a special mission had to be sent from Brussels to resolve the issue.

But food aid delays were of less consequence than ineffective European efforts to help restore the railway system. An experienced British railway consultant reported on what was needed at the end of 1984, and British companies were tendering for contracts in January 1985. It was not until June – again at British prompting – that a £6 million project was approved for the renovation of sixteen locomotives and other equipment. Commission officials in Brussels claimed that when the project was finally considered by the Council of Ministers at the end of May, a European record was established in gaining final approval. They also pointed out that other European nations had resented British encouragement for a project that was to benefit British companies. But the delay of five months had crucially impaired the value of the project. By the time work started, the 1985 rains were well advanced, and Sudan Railways a lost cause.

United Nations agencies were desperately slow on the uptake in Sudan. With a laggard Government in Khartoum unwilling to appeal for international help, the UN system was hamstrung. The UN's Food and Agricultural Organization consistently under-estimated the country's food needs – in comparison with American estimates which were remarkably accurate – and as late as 17 December 1984, Sudan received no mention from Edouard Saouma, Director-General of the FAO, when he listed the countries most gravely affected by famine. As in Ethiopia, there was an extraordinary three-month delay in the publication of an FAO mission report on food needs. The mission travelled to Sudan in November 1984, but recommendations were not made available to donors until February 1985.

When in doubt, set up a new UN office. In June 1985, Winston Prattley, a bristling New Zealander who was the senior regional official for the United Nations Development Programme in south-east Asia, was given the role of co-ordinating the relief effort in Sudan. He was to be the Kurt Jansson of Khartoum. His was the second full-time field appointment of the new Office for Emergency Operations in Africa, and it meant the abrupt removal of the quiet but widely respected Arthur Holcombe who, as resident representative of UNDP, was supposedly acting as local co-ordinator for the UN system. Once again the appointment was justified as 'elevating the level of command', but there was a crucial difference between Ethiopia and Sudan which further called into question the UN role. In Ethiopia, United Nations agencies were major players in the relief operation, and a co-ordination role was needed for the many Western aid agencies that belatedly came to the country's rescue. But how was the United Nations to co-ordinate a relief operation that was overwhelmingly dominated by one donor, the United States?

Prattley was unimpressed by the US performance. By the time he arrived in Khartoum, the second Arkel-Talab contract was already in crisis, and his plan was to start again from scratch. He would create UNSERO – the UN Sudan Emergency Relief Office. The UN would create its own truck fleet and invite private Sudanese truck operators to enter into fresh contracts with his organization. It did not work out like that because the United Nations never had the funds to compete with USAID, it never had the food, and it did not get its own modest truck fleet operational until much later in the year. American officials were also well aware of the breakdown in the West, and set out to remedy it. It was USAID which arranged the shipping of more trucks from Kuwait to strengthen the cross-desert operation to the west, and it was USAID which arranged for United States helicopters to carry food to the least accessible communities. Privately the Americans derided the UN's co-ordinating role in the emergency. 'Prattley can deal with the other donors if he wants,' said a senior American official. 'He doesn't deal with us.'

United Nations officials remained pointedly critical of the United States operation. They formally castigated reliance on Sudan Railways 'as a serious misjudgement of calamitous proportions', and stated further: 'To approach another season of famine in the belated, haphazard, irresponsible manner which has characterized efforts this year would constitute unconscionable negligence on the part of all concerned.' However justified, such criticism should not divert attention from the wholesale failure of the United Nations in Sudan.

The inadequacies of the United Nations operation in the early months of the Sudan crisis obliged USAID to look to the private agencies as major partners in food distribution. It was proof of how swiftly the voluntary agencies had been propelled to the forefront of international relief operations. From a small immunization programme in western Sudan, Save the Children Fund now found itself in sole charge of distributing food in a territory the size of England and

Wales. For SCF, the size of the Sudanese operation outstripped the rest of their worldwide activities put together. In capital equipment alone – trucks, workshops, and spare parts – it was valued at almost £5 million, and the agency had become an employer of thirty expatriates and 450 Sudanese.

There were dangers in assuming such huge responsibilities. Would private agencies become as bureaucratic as their official cousins? Would they forfeit their capacity to goad the big agencies into action? The implications of SCF's Topsy-like growth in Sudan were considered and approved at the agency's London headquarters. 'The British public didn't give us their money to sit on our hands,' said Mark Bowden, deputy director of the Overseas Department with responsibility for the African operation. 'They wanted us to get on with the job. We have approached it warily, but it would have been a breach of faith not to have gone ahead.'

In the field, difficulties in bringing relief to Darfur's scattered and hungry population remained as intractable as ever. To problems of weather, transport and food supply was added another – widespread corruption. Sudan's merchants are the country's most powerful class, and relief tends to be seen as another commodity to be supplied when profits can be assured, and denied when rewards are poor.

When I visited El Geneina, Save the Children was battling to redirect the energies of both local merchants and the local administration to the business of saving lives. It was an uphill struggle. Too much of the relief grain that did make it as far as the town was being cornered for distribution to Government servants, a privileged class. In the refugee camps, officials were insisting on working to grossly inflated figures even when many camp-dwellers had left for the planting season. There were incidents witnessed by foreign relief workers in which food that was supposed to be distributed in the camps was encountered by the truckload on the way back to town. And the need of outside agencies to get food to the worst affected drove transport prices through the roof as contractors played one agency off against another.

Peter Verney, Save the Children's field officer in El Geneina, recounted an exchange he had had that day with one of the town's hauliers. Verney was desperate to respond to the appeal he had received from the village of Beida for food and for shrouds to bury the dead. He offered the truck owner an already inflated price for the

171

journey, and was turned down. 'If you don't agree to take the food you will have the deaths of many children on your conscience,' Verney told him. 'That's not my business,' the contractor replied. Biting his lip to control his anger, Peter Verney told me: 'You would think it was just a normal business deal. They don't act as though there are lives at risk.'

Sudan was no advertisement for private enterprise. Despite massive American aid, President Numeiry had brought the country to a state of near-total economic collapse. By delaying international appeals for help, his Government had been additionally negligent. The successor régime of General Swar el Dahab proclaimed its good intentions, but found it almost impossible to mobilize the country's private sector transport and supposedly public sector railways to bring relief to the West. Over the Arkel-Talab contract, the greatest power on earth had been defeated by Sudanese conditions. Yet the bizarre view persisted that famine was a function of ideology. In a House of Lords debate in March 1985, the right-wing economist Lord Harris of High Cross asked: 'Why does the weather always seem to be so much worse in socialist countries?' It was an observation evidently directed against Ethiopia. His Lordship could usefully have studied the weather, political and otherwise, in Sudan.

14

Jumping to Conclusions

Much of Africa is in a profound crisis, and starvation is its index. For Africa's people, the dimensions of the crisis can easily be sketched. Africa's death rates are the highest in the world; life expectancy is the lowest. One in five Africans eats less than the minimum required for reasonable health; one in five children dies before their first birthday; one in 200 Africans is a refugee. 'Africa is a disaster zone,' said a West African development minister in 1985. 'Africa no longer has the means to assure its existence.'

For the nation states of Africa, the crisis goes equally deep. In the words of an American official, 'Africa is in an economic tailspin.' In the 1960s and 1970s food production declined by a fifth, and now a fifth of all food imports arrives as aid. If Africa's population continues to rise and food production does not rise to meet it, the continent will feed only two in five of its people by the year 2000. African indebtedness to the bankers of the developed world is spiralling; interest payments will have risen from around $2 billion at the beginning of the decade to $8 billion in 1986, thus neutralizing aid commitments. Terms of trade have moved against the African producer: a ton of cocoa that fetched £3,000 in 1977 fetched £800 in 1982, and because of oil price rises and inflation in the industrialized world, that £800 only bought £300 worth of goods at 1977 prices. All this happened in a continent that in twenty years had seen twelve wars, fifty coups and the assassination of thirteen heads of state. In startling language for a United Nations report, the Economic Commission for Africa foresaw 'almost a nightmare' by the year 2000.

As the African emergency escalated, a debate flourished in aid circles as to who or what was responsible. There were those who maintained that the crisis was the result of wrong-headed economic policies pursued by African Governments, and that much Western aid was accordingly misplaced. The opposing school of thought pinned all the blame on the rich world. Damage not wrought by colonialism was

173

put down to 'neo-colonialism'. The Western world had to reform its policies towards the Third World and aid had to be substantially increased.

Even this important debate was overtaken by the enormity of the suffering that was witnessed first in Ethiopia in 1984, then in Sudan and elsewhere in 1985. What rapidly emerged was a new consensus among the aid experts that would guarantee them a role for another generation. The right-wingers had apparently been correct all along: much official aid had been inappropriate and misdirected; there had to be a fresh aid revolution.

Small was now beautiful. The white elephants that roamed the African bush were to be rendered extinct. Even the World Bank, largest of all the aid-givers, expanded on the theme. 'Financing big infrastructure projects has represented a large part of past donor programmes. These programmes must be re-examined,' said its report 'Toward Sustained Development in Sub-Saharan Africa', published in August 1984. The Bank proposed abandoning large projects in mid-course. No argument was brooked on the new view. 'The new emerging consensus on policy issues dwarfs any remaining areas of dissent,' the Bank said. 'Delay in taking action, whether by African Governments or donors, can no longer be justified on the grounds of major disagreements in diagnosis and prescription.'

Ethiopia had never fitted comfortably into other people's stereotypes. European colonizers were in control of the country for only five years, and not even the most dedicated anti-imperialist could maintain that Italian rule had dictated the next forty years of the country's misfortunes. Grisly famines had been regular visitors to the Ethiopian highlands long before they could be blamed on outsiders. Early travellers had recorded in words what television captured in pictures in 1984. 'We are accosted for help and, from their death beds, suddenly rise a mob of skeletons whose bones can be seen under their taut skin,' recorded an Italian diplomat at the time of the Great Famine in 1891. 'I flee to escape from it and stumble on young boys searching in the excrement of camels to find a grain of dura.'

By the 1980s the country was resolutely out of step with the new thinking on aid from the West. A document prepared in 1985 for the World Food Council, the United Nations 'think tank' on food matters, could have been written with Ethiopia in mind. 'A number of observers have argued that domestic policies in most African countries are extremely hostile to improved food and agricultural production – producers faced with a plethora of disincentives: low producer prices, unreliable delivery of inputs like fertilizer, poor marketing services, plus a parasitic and mismanaged public sector.' In addition to disincentives to small farmers, Ethiopia insisted on devoting the lion's share of development resources to wasteful and inefficient state farms which were responsible for only a tiny proportion of the country's production.

There seemed little chance of an economic change of heart. The United Nations declared Ethiopia to be in the 'initial stages' of formulating a food strategy – which meant that the country had hardly begun. Big remained beautiful for the Ethiopian leadership and its Soviet allies. Ethiopia's military dependence on the Soviet Union probably precluded its planners from following a more liberal policy. Early on in the revolution, Colonel Mengistu stated that it had been 'shown in practice that collective enterprise leads to greater production than individualistic effort'. State farms 'should become the backbone of our national economy'. If Ethiopian officials were less inclined in 1985 to emphasize the dubious merits of Soviet-style agriculture, their Russian backers were not. A Soviet *New Times* commentary in January 1985 extolled the Soviet tractor plant and storage and refrigeration plants being built in Ethiopia. 'It is the long-term, versatile large-scale technical and economic co-operation, and not one-time donations, that is vitally important to Ethiopia.'

For all the waywardness of its economic policy, Ethiopia needed creative and positive assistance from the West. Before the famine, Ethiopia received an annual $6 per head in overseas aid. This compared with $20 per head received by the rest of Black Africa. The huge relief operation contributed a further $12 per head to Ethiopia, but that only served to emphasize how little assistance the country received for endeavours other than keeping its people alive. 'It is too early to say whether the increased interest of donors in Ethiopia, due to the drought disaster, will be successful in generating significantly increased concessionary aid for long-term development,' commented the World Bank.

By the middle of 1985, it was clear that the West's big aid-givers were not going to make substantial additional commitments to agricultural development in Ethiopia or anywhere else in Africa. Under public pressure, Western Governments had managed to bring starving people back up to the breadline, but that is where they were to be left. At pledging conferences for donors in Geneva and Rome in 1985, the outcome was the same: that food would be provided in abundance from surpluses held in the West, but there would be no corresponding generosity in the task of making Africa self-reliant. Four months after its big donor conference in Geneva in March, the United Nations Office for Emergency Operations in Africa calculated that $1.17 billion had been pledged in food, but only $112 million in non-food items like seeds, tools and pesticides. The unmet non-food needs were still put at more than $500 million. According to Bradford Morse, head of the OEOA, the imbalance in Western contributions 'defied logic'. The American campaigning group Bread for the World calculated that it cost $400 to send one tonne of famine relief to Africa, but with the right sort of development assistance farmers could at half the cost grow one tonne of food a year for the rest of their lives.

Behind the failure to make adequate commitments to development lay a growing hostility on the part of the United States and some of its close allies towards United Nations agencies. We have seen why the Food and Agricultural Organization in Rome was mistrusted, but this attitude extended to agencies that were regularly praised by Western Governments and whose operations were in keeping with the new approach to development. The World Bank's 'Special Facility for Africa', for instance, was aimed in part at securing reforms in African states still wedded to illiberal agricultural policies. The Bank originally aimed for a fund of $2 billion, but had to be content, 'considering the generally difficult environment for aid', with $1.1 billion. The United States did not contribute at all, and Britain's modest contribution was pledged only 'in association' with the Bank's fund.

If any single United Nations agency deserved backing in the African emergency, it was the International Fund for Agricultural Development (IFAD) based, along with the bigger UN agricultural agencies, in Rome. IFAD was another product of the explosion of international concern about world hunger in 1974. With a system of small-scale loans aimed at subsistence farmers, this was 'do-it-yourself' development in action. IFAD was described by a United States Ambassador as 'the most American of all the programmes' and received regular endorsement from USAID: 'IFAD's major strength in the policy area is its commitment to focussing the attention of other donors and host Governments on the needs and capacities of the rural poor,' said AID.

Yet American action in the course of 1985 brought IFAD to its knees.

IFAD was funded through an imaginative partnership between the industrialized and oil-producing countries. The oil producers had money to spare in the 1970s and their contributions were in part penance for the damage that their price rises had inflicted on fragile Third World economies. By the mid-1980s the oil bubble had burst, and the oil producers looked more cautiously at IFAD's next request for funds. Already the agency had regretfully halved its programme; what remained at issue was the proportion that the industrialized and the oil-producing countries would contribute.

The debate was fitfully staged during a series of international conferences in 1984 and 1985, as Africa starved. The United States wanted a 52:48 per cent share-out, with the industrialized countries contributing the bare majority of funds; IFAD proposed a 60:40 per cent breakdown and received everyone else's agreement, including the other industrialized nations. But the Americans erected a few percentage points into major points of principle, and for months IFAD was threatened with bankruptcy. The difference between the two propositions would cost the United States $2.5 million; it was a small sum on which to break the Administration's favourite UN agency.

Washington's attitude towards the multilateral agencies was part of a whole new strategic approach towards aid for Africa. Its philosophical underpinning was cogently articulated by the right-wing think-tank the Heritage Foundation. In its 'Mandate for Leadership II', sub-titled 'Continuing the Conservative Revolution', published in 1984, the foundation stated that humanitarian assistance to African countries should continue regardless of their alignment, but that there should be much more picking and choosing in the application of economic aid. 'Only Governments that use the market to encourage food production in rural areas and allow private industry and investment to operate should receive significant American assistance.' Countries like Ethiopia would be the losers. 'The United States should know by now that attempts to use aid and other incentives to make marginal gains with generally hostile nations should not take priority over improving ties with more friendly Governments.'

This thinking found expression in President Reagan's Economic Policy Initiative for Africa. With a price tag of $500 million over five years, this was to be a more aggressive version of the World Bank's Fund. The money would be spent on providing additional support for countries adopting 'dynamic', that is private enterprise-oriented, economic policies. There was no guarantee that the policy would be either to the benefit of the poorest countries or even to the advantage of the poorest within those countries assisted. It was directed at gaining and sustaining new friends.

There was more help forthcoming from the United States military. From the 1960s, the Soviet Union had been the dominant supplier of weaponry to Black Africa. With the development of the United States Rapid Deployment Force, the Americans began to get on level pegging with their Soviet rivals. It was no accident that the three countries bordering Ethiopia – Sudan, Kenya and Somalia – should be among the principal recipients of increased United States military assistance. Congressional concern was expressed at the way in which such increases in military aid were dwarfing additional economic commitments. Congressman Byron Dorgan from North Dakota made the point well in November 1983: 'I don't see how Africa can afford to be militarized when it already has the same number of soldiers as the US, but only one-eighth of the number of physicians, barely half our life expectancy rates, and two-thirds of the people consuming less than the recommended national calorific standard.'

Some disputed the political wisdom of directing aid away from America's supposed enemies in Africa towards her supposed friends. Ken Hackett, regional director for Sub-Saharan Africa for Catholic Relief Services, told the same Congressional hearing: 'To isolate countries because a specific Government espouses an ideal that clashes with our own is short-sighted. Punishing the starving because an oligarchy, under the pseudonym of "People's Democratic Republic" or whatever, in no way serves our long-term interests ... We are closing ourselves out of many of the political processes of Africa because we are delineating friends and foes.'

The militarization of Africa and the co-opting of African states into a strategic struggle were only the most potent symbols of a relationship that had gone badly awry. One hundred years before the African famine, in December 1884, representatives of Europe's great powers met in Berlin to carve up the continent. This was the scramble for Africa, spuriously sanctified as the Berlin Conference. A century later it was easy to look back in horror at what had been done in the earlier association between Europe and Africa. What succeeded it was supposedly done in the name of partnership and development for a better world. The results seemed just as degrading.

Two decades of 'development' brought Africa to the precipice in 1984. It then finally dawned that the process had been a sham. Africa's rural people had been left out of account by an official aid community that dealt with Governments, and by Governments that regularly ignored the interests of its people. 'Development' continued as people starved to death.

The overseas 'development' community was supplanted in Africa in 1984 and 1985 by the overseas 'disaster' community. In their own self-deprecating terms, these were Africa's 'Masters of Disaster', the continent's 'Soldiers of Misfortune'. Their cynicism began to rival that of journalists. I even heard one group talk about a modern-day Conference of Berlin at which relief agencies had divided up an African country between them. Here was the latest manifestation of an historical process that began with slavery. Unhealthy dependence was being perpetuated.

What was urgently needed was fresh examination of the entire 'aid' relationship, leading perhaps to its termination. Over a period, Africa without aid could scarcely be in a worse state than Africa with aid. A cessation of aid might even embolden those who had never benefited to start imposing their wishes on those who ruled them. That such a worthy objective was not discussed during the months of international exposure to Africa's degradation is evidence of the entrenched interests in the 'aid' equation. On the one hand, many African régimes depend for their political survival on 'aid'; on the other, there is a large body of professionals in the developed world who depend for their livelihood upon continuing the 'aid' relationship.

To postulate disengagement also clarifies the relationship between rich and poor countries. The notion that Western aid is humanitarian in motive has long been questioned, and the new realism expressed in such capitals as Washington and London has finally exploded it. But the flow of 'aid' funds is only part of the equation. Whose industries benefit from continuing under-development in the Third World? Whose consumers benefit from primary products that keep African producers just above the bread-line? Whose bankers benefit from Third World indebtedness? Whose arms manufacturers benefit from African arms races? Whose delicate consciences are soothed by the giving of modest gifts?

Since immediate disengagement is neither desirable nor feasible, a realistic starting point might be an honest acknowledgement of the aid community's failure to avert widespread death by starvation in 1984. For if the aid-givers failed even to keep people alive, how likely is it that they would manage to improve people's livelihood? In the aftermath of famine, the top aid professionals moved with astonishing speed to adopt the new 'small is beautiful' approach to development. This was done without any fresh appraisal of the real constraints on development, and outsiders were once again enthusiastically imposing their own ideas.

In my visits to some of the world's major aid bureaucracies, I was struck by the number of times I was told of records being broken in such and such an institution's response to the famine – or at least to television's account of the famine. Even the respected International Fund for Agricultural Development in Rome spoke of 'a sort of world record' in approving a drought rehabilitation project for Ethiopia. It had been identified in December 1984, appraised in January 1985, and approved by the IFAD board in April. What this meant was that experts from IFAD and experts from the Ethiopian Government had got together in a hurry to draw up an entirely worthy $20 million programme to provide seeds and hand tools for some of the famine areas. Notable for their lack of involvement in this process of consultation were the famine-affected farmers themselves.

If an aid moratorium, even a short one, were ever introduced, the grace period could best be used in hearing and considering the views of African subsistence farmers. These are the real experts in scratching a living from Africa's soil, and it may be time that they were involved in plans for their own future. The veterinary approach to development, which takes no formal account of the wishes of its supposed beneficiaries, should be no part of the new consensus on aid.

Epilogue: Korem 1985

I returned to Korem on 19 June 1985, aboard one of those flying circuses arranged for visiting VIPs. Christian Nucci, the French Minister of Co-operation and Development, was being shown the sights of starvation along with other French officials and a travelling press corps from Paris. First we flew by helicopter to watch an air-drop, then on to an airfield in southern Wollo. Here we transferred to an old Dakota for the flight to an airstrip at the foot of the Korem escarpment. Vehicles were waiting to take us up the hill, through the town, and to the relief camp.

It was better ordered than I remembered it in October 1984. There were new corrugated-iron shelters for the most malnourished, one prominently marked 'Starvation Room'. The death rate, which was topping 100 a day when I last visited, was now down to twenty. Western food aid had made the difference between life and death for thousands of people who sought help from dedicated Ethiopian and foreign relief workers in the camp. But keeping people alive was all that had been achieved.

The 52,000 people at Korem were prisoners in their relief camp. They had neither the means nor the opportunity to resume a productive life. The Government was able to manage only erratic food supplies to the camp. This meant that food could never be distributed in enough quantity to allow people to go home and start planting. Even if the food had been there, there was neither the seed nor the fertilizer nor the basic agricultural tools to enable the farmers to sow. The West had been begged for these items, but for months some of the biggest donors agonized over whether to provide such 'development' assistance to Marxists. The little that was committed in 1985 arrived too late – the everyday story of Western aid.

The French Ministerial party allowed forty minutes for its tour of Korem. Like so many other VIPs before him, Nucci was moved by what he saw in the makeshift medical wards run by the excellent French doctors of Médecins Sans Frontières. 'It touches my heart,' he said, banging his chest. It was a sentiment only slightly debased by his anxiety to conduct a politician's hand-shaking tour of the starving for the benefit of French TV.

Among his officials there was no inclination to examine afresh the needs of Korem and a score of places like it. France had given its 16,500 tonnes of food aid to Ethiopia, and its officials had calculated to the last decimal point its share of European Community assistance – 23.6 per cent, to be precise. No mention was made of the 100,000 tonnes of grain that France had just sold to Ethiopia for $15 million. Even in the matter of food shipments, there are benefits to the West.

'What is the answer to this?' I asked a very clever French official as we drove through Korem's sea of imprisoned humanity. 'That depends on the question,' he replied. 'Well, the West has helped keep these people alive and that must be good, but what are we doing to allow them to break out of this terrible crisis?' The French official replied: 'Look, 90 per cent of the problem is the weather, and we can't control that. Of the remaining 10 per cent, 9 per cent of responsibility must continue to rest here in this country. For foreigners, ours is only the remaining 1 per cent of responsibility.'

With disclaimers like that, it is no wonder that Western leaders have scaled down their plans for eliminating starvation. Henry Kissinger's 'bold objective' that by 1984 no child would go to bed hungry was quietly abandoned during the decade. Ministers who met at the World Food Council in Addis Ababa in 1984 spoke only of the international community renewing its commitment 'to eradicate hunger and malnutrition as soon as possible, and by no later than the end of the century'. Even the offspring of Kissinger's hungry child would have to wait.

When Christian Nucci had shaken the hand of every French relief worker in Korem, our convoy set off to catch the Dakota back to Addis Ababa. The Minister had a meeting with a member of the Ethiopian Politburo before boarding his executive jet for Paris. Halfway down the Korem escarpment, French TV asked to stop. As we had done in October 1984, the cameraman wanted a shot of the spectacular hairpin bends that food convoys had to negotiate on their way to the relief camp. This was the spot where I had met the family on the road – resourceful father, mother carrying her baby boy, whimpering daughter and lame grandmother. No one was by the roadside that afternoon. But I fear they will return.

Chronology: Famine in Ethiopia

1982

December   Save the Children Fund opens feeding centre in Korem. Catholic Relief Services ask United States Government for 838 tonnes of food for Ethiopian emergency.

1983

March   1,000 children on emergency feeding in Korem. *Sunday Times* of London claims emergency food aid for Ethiopia diverted to Soviet Union.

April   Save the Children Fund team in Korem kidnapped.

May   United Nations Food and Agriculture Organization appeals for help for 22 African countries. United Nations Food and Agriculture Organization for Ethiopia after five months' delay.

June   World Food Programme official estimates 50 to 100 children dying daily in northern Ethiopia.

September   Save the Children Fund restarts feeding centre in Korem.

October   Catholic Relief Services ask United States Government for 16,000 tonnes of emergency food.

November   90 per cent crop failure predicted in parts of northern Ethiopia. Meeting in London between Ethiopian relief commissioner and British aid Minister; British allege misuse of aid.

December   2,000 children on emergency feeding in Korem.

1984

January   United States Administration announces $90 million additional aid for Africa.

February   United Nations sends special mission to Ethiopia to assess food needs.

March   6,000 children on emergency feeding in Korem. Ethiopian Ministerial committee formed on 'drought'. Colonel Mengistu leaves for Moscow. United States Senate votes $150 million extra for Africa, but money made contingent on approval of

	military funds for Central America.

military funds for Central America.

Ethiopian Relief Commission appeals for 450,000 tonnes of emergency food for five million people.

April $90 million in additional United States aid for Africa becomes law.

May   15,000 destitutes in Korem.

Ethiopian Relief Commissioner meets British Foreign Office Minister; no significant British commitment.

Senior United Nations official in Ethiopia describes UN response to famine as 'an exercise in cynicism'.

United States Government approves 8,000 tonnes of emergency food for Ethiopia after seven months' delay.

European Community responds to Ethiopian request for 115,000 tonnes of food by converting 18,000 tonnes development grant to emergency use.

Ethiopia requests 26,000 tonnes of emergency food through World Food Programme.

June   8,000 children on emergency feeding in Korem.

United Nations World Food Conference meets in Addis Ababa.

Edouard Saouma, director-general of UN Food and Agriculture Organization, delays clearance of emergency food request for Ethiopia.

United Nations special mission report published; appeals for only 125,000 tonnes of emergency food.

Mrs Thatcher hosts London Economic Summit; communiqué states that leaders are 'greatly concerned' about African drought, and are pledged 'to maintain and wherever possible increase' aid to Africa.

July   Oxfam issues warnings on famine in guerrilla-held Tigre; 8,000 starvation deaths in six months.

$60 million in additional US aid to Africa becomes law after four months' delay, but funds linked to military aid to El Salvador.

'Seeds of Despair' transmitted on British Independent Television.

August   400 die in Korem feeding centre during the month.

Ethiopian television opens new transmitter in famine area.

	Colonel Mengistu opens tractor assembly plant and cement factory.
	United Nations puts Ethiopian food gap at only 50,000 tonnes.
	USAID reassures Congress on Ethiopian food needs.
September	40 a day dying in Korem.
	Founding Congress of Workers' Party of Ethiopia.
	Celebration of tenth anniversary of Ethiopian revolution.
	United Nations agency says 'almost satisfactory growing conditions' in main crop areas.
	Oxfam announces 10,000-tonne grain shipment to shame Western governments into action.
	18 private agencies in Addis Ababa demand 'immediate and extraordinary action' from Western donors.
October	100 a day dying in Korem.
	British television teams allowed to travel to famine areas.
	British Government seeks space on Oxfam grain ship.
	BBC TV news reports on famine; world opinion stirs.

Index

187

188